D1498010

day trade futures online

Wiley Online Trading for a Living

Electronic Day Trading to Win / Bob Baird and Craig McBurney

The Strategic Electronic Day Trader/Robert Deel

Day Trade Online/Christopher A. Farrell

Trade Options Online/George A. Fontanills

Electronic Day Trading 101/Sunny J. Harris

Trade Stocks Online/Mark L. Larson

How I Trade for a Living/Gary Smith

Day Trade Futures Online/Larry Williams

Trade IPOs Online/Matthew D. Zito and Matt Olejarczyk

day
trade
futures
online

LARRY WILLIAMS

John Wiley & Sons, Inc.
New York · Chichester · Weinheim · Brisbane · Singapore · Toronto

Published by John Wiley & Sons, Inc.

Published simultaneously in Canada.

Portions of this book have been reproduced from *Long-Term Secrets to Short-Term Trading* by Larry Williams, copyright © 1999 by Larry Williams. Reprinted by permission of John Wiley & Sons, Inc.

Navigator charts were provided by
Genesis Financial Data Services: 800-808-3282.

This publication is designed to provide accurate and authoritative information in regard to the subject matter covered. It is sold with the understanding that the publisher is not engaged in rendering professional services. If professional advice or other expert assistance is required, the services of a competent professional person should be sought.

Library of Congress Cataloging-in-Publication Data:

Williams, Larry R.
    Day trade futures online / Larry Williams.
        p. cm. — (Wiley online trading for a living)
    Includes index.
    ISBN 0-471-38339-2 (cloth : alk. paper)
        1. Day trading (Securities) I. Title. II. Series.
    HG4515.95.W55 2000
    323.64′5—dc21

                                                    00-027520

10 9 8 7 6 5 4 3 2 1

acknowledgments

It's funny how we authors dedicate our books to family and loved ones, who, for the most part care little about what we write and seldom read it anyway.

That's why this book is dedicated to the many people who have supported me in my endeavors: the folks who have stood by me through thick and thin and have been with me for the good and bad times, and those people who have helped me better understand myself or the markets.

The first person to ever show me such support was Gill Haller, a true iconoclast and market analyst about 30 years ahead of his time. While I appreciated the wisdom he shared with me, I also learned from him to support and assist other people. There was no earthly reason for Gill to encourage me, to spend or waste time with me. But he did, because that was his style, to be positive. Years went by before I was able to sum all human action into one of two categories, that of expanding your love or contracting it. Gill chose to expand, to help. I owe you, Gill, and have tried to repay that debt by treating others as you treated me.

Tom DeMark has been a close and personal friend—hell, a real buddy—over some 20 years. He has pushed me to learn more about the markets and has humored me to live through my financial as well as personal "drawdowns." But above all, his steadfast support and even defense of me, made me better grasp what my mission as a trader and teacher is all about. I also owe Tom, as well as his wonderful wife Nancy, for our mutual friend Pam Johnson, who has opened doors I had closed long ago.

Other friends who have been supportive are Richard Joseph, Harvey Levine, Jim Vidal, Brian Cloutier, and Jeff Swenson.

Without my brokers I would not be able to trade, so you know I owe them! I owe them for not getting in my face at the wrong time, and for not telling me what they think or what their firm is touting. They have been there to answer the questions I asked, to take my orders, and to execute them. I am saddened to see computers replace brokers and the very long-term relationships that have developed across two and three generations of dealing with my brokers. Brokers I "owe" are Al Allesandra and his son and protégé, Greg, the first guys I traded with on a big-time basis. Additionally, I am grateful to Joe Miller, my first broker, for not laughing at my foolish attempts to break the bank.

Ed Walters has provided me with daily commodity quotes, jokes, and data for longer than either of us care to remember. He's been the most consistent part of my trading. I'm also a big fan of Joel Robbins and Larry Herst of Robbins Brokerage. Not only did they believe in me when the stupid National Futures Association (NFA) singled me out for "cruel and unusual punishment," but Joel, who could have walked away from the battle, stayed the course, giving me full support at a time most others would have crumbled to the bureaucratic nightmare. That's just one reason why I also trade with Robbins.

Andy Daniels, with the firm of Linnco Futures Group (LFG), has also been a strong supporter and a person willing to play the game straight up—win, lose, or draw. He has walked his talk with me, time and time again, and his brokers have done a good job of filling my orders.

My absolute knowledge of the markets would have remained sophomoric had it not been for Bill Cruz developing System Writer and TradeStation, the first and finest research software packages in the marketplace. Bill's ability to be patient with me while I learned how to use a computer and software still amazes me.

Glen Larsen at Genesis Data revolutionized my life with his service that allows one to download all markets at the end of each trading day. No longer do I need to call Ed to get the open, high, low, close, volume open, interest, and so on, for each of the markets I monitor. In the old days I had to do that daily, recording those numbers in my notebook, then "running the numbers" to construct the tools I use before plotting them in my chart book. Glen, you made me a happy camper and shortened my workday by about 2 hours, which must have extended my life.

The list of fellow traders and advisers that I want to acknowledge always begins with Bill Meehan, a kindly old guy who taught me more than he realized about markets and life, and importantly began me on my personal journey to optimum health. Others have been my long-time friend Jake Bernstein who has also seen me through thick and thin and has personally increased everyone's understanding of the markets with his seasonal studies.

I want especially to thank Miles Dunbar for helping me research and write about the technical aspects of the Internet and computers that are discussed in Chapter 1, "What You Need to Get Started." I'm certain traders will hear more from Miles in the years to come.

The long list of people who have helped me includes Lee Gettes, Steve Moore, Joe DiNapoli, Bob Baird, Don Southard, Curt Hessler, Linda Bradford Raschke, Courtney Smith, Ron Michaelsen, Bob Miller, Larry McMillan, Murray Ruggiero, Bob Prechter, Nelson Freeburg, Ralph Vince, Ryan Jones, Tim Mather of CQG fame, and Frank Toucher, who led the battle for freedom of the press for letter writers and speakers. The list goes on . . . showing how much I have learned from other people. There are many more, just not enough space for all of them. No man is an island, especially when it comes to gaining more knowledge, something I am always looking for anywhere and everywhere. At this stage in my life, I am particularly interested in what is not true, whose theories and ideas do not work.

Some of the modalities that have made me what I am, or am not, come from psychological views. That would include long sessions at Esalen many years ago and my early ministers in the Presbyterian church in Billings, Montana: Werner Erhardt, Tony Robbins, and fellow Montanan L. Ron Hubbard. From Alan Watts to Joseph Campbell, Carl Sagan to Carlos Castenada, and the Zurich Axioms to Dale Carnegie, I have been able to sample a great many different approaches to life that have helped when market and life pressures have collided full steam ahead.

I want also to thank my editor at John Wiley & Sons, Pamela van Giessen, for insisting this book see the light of day and for the tremendous help Claudio Campuzano, her assistant editor, gave in bringing this concept to print. Kim Henrie of British American deserves heartfelt thanks for bringing my video course to the marketplace as well.

Tired of all this? I hope not. These people played a part in getting me to the point I'm at today so I can show you how to really make money trading, which this book will do. Finally, I want to thank and acknowledge the some 50,000 students all over the world, who now read my work in English, Chinese, Japanese, Russian, and German. Without readers, there would never be authors, so I am grateful to all of you for your fascination with the markets and with my theories of how and why they work.

That's who this book is really dedicated to . . . you.

L. W.

contents

introduction

Day trading used to be the domain of the floor traders at the futures exchanges—the "locals." They are the ones who can take the best advantage of price volatility to increase profits. For one, they don't pay commissions. For another, they have access to up-to-the-second price information, including bid-and-ask information. And they can sense the mood of the pits. Even in this online age, the locals still have these advantages over the rest of us, but it is diminishing: commissions and exchange fees keep going down (and many brokers offer a discount to day traders because they don't have to fully report positions that were opened and closed in the same day); real-time news and quotes are a reality for the online community; electronic order entry systems are available that send orders straight to the floor in many markets; and although the mood of the pit is still unknown to outsiders, so many resources are available to us online that we can make up with them what we lose by not being in the pits.

All this said, I am more inclined to trade over the short term—usually my trades last one to four days. Even as their advantages diminish, the locals still own the scalping game, so I believe the most profitable method for the online trader is position trading. This book, however, is for all futures traders who work in a less than a long-term time horizon. While most of my examples are of interday trades, many of the concepts can be applied to intraday trades. What I offer are not cut-and-dried systems; they are ideas that can be used separately or in combination to build a system that works for you—one that trades as frequently or as infrequently as you would like. I encourage you to take the ideas that I offer—that come from decades as a participant in the futures market—and build and test your own system, whether you use daily bars or one-minute bars. Building a trading system is as much about the personality of the trader as it is about results. Don't just trade what works on paper. Trade what works for *you* in the real world. And short-term trading has worked for me.

Taking positions over the span of a few days, I have found, allows me to take fuller advantage of an advantageous move in price. That is what the futures game is all about—waiting to enter a sideways market until a swing in price is imminent (or just begun) and then riding that swing until it starts to fail. Closing out positions at the end of the day just because it is the end of the day, to me, does not seem like a logical exit strategy. But I've been playing this game for a long time, and I am used to the feeling of holding a position overnight. For those new to the game: it isn't so bad. But if you need to close out positions at the end of the day in order to sleep at night, that is your personality, and you need to trade that way. If you believe that adverse movement at the open of the next day or succeeding days is just as likely as beneficial movement at the open, then that is the way you need to trade. Among other things, this is a game of psychology, so don't try to trade a system that is counter to your psychological makeup.

Why the Futures Market Is Well Suited to Day Trading and Short-Term Trading

Whether you decide to tackle this game as a short-term trader or day trader, you'll find that this is one of the best games in town. Why? Futures is the original short-term game. Recently, stock trading has been all the rage. That is because there has been a lot of media hype and skyrocketing, supervolatile stock prices. Anyone can play and win with no stock-picking ability and no money management skill if prices are always going up. With minimal leverage, you can get in and out of the market and have some extra cash to take home in the short term. But what happens when this volatility disappears? Getting in and out in a day—or even a week—is going to cost you much more in brokers' commissions than you are going to make on a point move. Even if you leverage yourself to the max (50 percent on stock trades), you aren't going to get too much bang for your buck.

The futures game really is not about the volatility of the prices, but the extreme effect of leverage. As a futures speculator, you become much more active, and your wins and losses compound much more quickly. In the futures markets, the ability to leverage with very little on margin allows the trader to make (and lose) more off smaller swings. Good or bad? It depends on who you are and how you like to play, but if you are a day trader or short-term trader, then you are looking to collapse your time frame for reaching your profit target or hitting your pain threshold. Is it riskier to hold a stock for a year that goes down by 50 percent than to hold a commodity future for a day that goes down 5 percent with 10 percent on margin? Same stuff, different pile. By collapsing your time frame, you compound your wins and losses more quickly. So in a sense, the volatility that everyone talks about in the futures game is not really price volatility. It is equity volatility.

This brings me to my next point.

My Most Important Market Belief

Based on my research and experience, I have developed a powerful and profitable belief system:

I believe my current trade will be a loser . . . a big loser at that.

This may sound pretty negative to all you positive thinkers, but positive thinking can give way to thinking you will win—a sure-fire formula for buying and selling too many contracts and holding on too long. After all, if you are positive things will work out, you are certain to hold for a bounce or turn that never comes.

If you get all pumped up and glossed over with positive beliefs about your market success, your conviction will lead you to mismanage losing trades. That is why belief systems are so important to a trader. If your belief system tells you the current trade will be a winner—and it isn't—the need to confirm that belief in your mind will literally force you to let losses run, to stay with losers, something no successful trader ever does. An outrageously positive belief that the next trade or two will turn your account around or make a small fortune for you is most dangerous.

Now let's look at my belief that my current trade will be a loser, that I have no pact with God for success on this trade. Indeed, I genuinely believe the market is not precisely perfect. Keep in mind the data for this belief overwhelmingly support it: 75 percent of mutual fund managers do not outperform the Dow; 80 percent of short-term traders lose their risk capital. On a personal note, many of my own trades do not make money, and I can positively guarantee many of yours will not succeed.

No major loss I have ever had, and I have had more than my fair share of them, has been the market's "fault." "They" were never out to get me. I persuaded myself my current trade would be a winner so I did not follow the rules of the game.

I agree with those who say you are only as powerful as your belief system because that belief will give you the power of taking an action with more certainty and less hesitation. We act out what we believe: Our beliefs are the scriptwriters for our play of life.

Adopt my belief that the current trade will most likely not work out and you sure as heck will protect yourself with stops. You will control disasters, taking the first lifeboat possible instead of going down with a sinking ship.

Adopt my belief that the current trade will most likely not work out and you sure as heck will not load up on a trade, banking on it to bail out all your problems. A tiny loss can wipe you out when you have taken a very large position.

Positive beliefs about future results cause us to take on undue risk. Doing that in a game where the odds are unfavorable to begin with is a sure invitation to disaster. The sooner you learn to master your defeats, the sooner you will be on your way to amass the wealth possible in this business. Your failures, not your successes, kill you in this business. Failures do not build character, they destroy your bank account.

The Beginning of My Career as a Speculator

From all that I have said in the preceding paragraphs, some people might wonder why I play this game at all. In fact, it is an important question for all speculators to ask themselves, because a deep understanding of yourself is integral to trading successfully. We all need to trade or invest in the way that best suits us. Here is some background so you know where I am coming from.

Everyone in Montana works hard. Certainly, my dad worked as hard as anyone, putting in over 40 hours a week at a refinery, then more hours on weekends at Doc Zinc's sulfur refinery. And as if that wasn't enough, he would stay up late at night reading books, taking courses on electronics so he would be more valuable to Conoco, his career employer. The gambit of hard work and loyalty paid off—he got promoted.

One of the advantages of having a father working at the refinery was that his kids could get summer jobs there if they were in college. I did that too, and it reinforced my strong desire to not do what these guys did: Work long hours with ever changing shift work. One week, you went to work at 3:30 P.M., the next week at 11:30 P.M., and the following week you might pull the 3:30 shift or start at 7:30 A.M. The schedules made no sense that I could see. All I registered was the unending hours of voluntary servitude in a hot, stench-filled, noisy refinery.

My general laziness coupled with a desire to be alone and a total inability to do anything well besides drawing, caused me to feel inadequate. My initial response to find self-esteem came from sports. But that sense of approval only lasts through the game. I would lay awake in bed dreaming, scheming about how to have a better life, wondering how the few people with really big houses achieved success. I was not content; what I wanted was a way out.

Making fake driver's licenses (for $5 each, birth certificates for $20) paid a lot better. My limited artistic talents made more money and let me work by myself. It also included a healthy dose of risk. I liked knowing that I was doing something the average person couldn't or wouldn't; and for sure, I was not going to find that kind of satisfaction in what I saw at the time as my father's humdrum existence. My dad did everything by the book and followed all the rules.

Really good speculators like thrill; indeed they seek it, as some sort of intellectual rush.

Maybe that is why I liked selling newspapers on the street corners after school or Christmas cards and garden seeds door-to-door to pick up spending money. I was at risk (while operating legally), never knowing if the time I was putting in was going to result in a sale. But I had the opportunity to make some decent money doing something I enjoyed that depended on my ability and that came easily: talking and showing some stuff.

I had seen enough hard work to know I did not covet it. Freckles Brown, a world champion bull rider once said, "I ride rodeo because I'm too lazy to work and too honest to steal." Going to college or joining the Navy after high school seemed to me to be the right direction, and it was one my mom and dad encouraged. They always told us to do better, that there was an easier life, and college was the door to that life.

In 1962, I asked someone what the "most active" list of stocks in the newspaper meant. I was hooked when he replied, "Well, see that stock for General Motors was up 1½ for the day? Had you bought it yesterday, you would have made $150 today."

$150 in one day!

Back then, $150 was more than guys at the refinery made in a week. This looked easy, and the winnings were staggering. My only two questions were, how did one get started and where had I been all my life? There was an instant affinity between me and what looked like easy money.

That affinity led to the greatest challenge of my life, something I have worked hard at just about every day since 1962. My only real "time off" from the markets occurred when I ran for U.S. Senate in 1978 and 1982. Other than those two interruptions, I have spent every day of my life "working"—much to my father's pleasure, I am certain—but it has never resembled the work at the refinery or jobs in and after college.

From this experience, I believe that three motivators stir the heart of a successful speculator: an intense desire to make a lot of money, a longing or yearning to show somebody else up, and an internal discontent with how things are. Great big chunks of unrest seem to be an important asset for a speculator. Although most people seek balance in their lives, I have never found that very healthy; no great achievements were ever made by perfectly normal people. Sometimes I think about living a more balanced life. That thought usually lasts a couple of seconds. I guess my unrest will never go away, but if my lifestyle tells us anything, it is that unrest fans the flames of a speculator's internal fires.

I would probably trade the markets without wanting profits if it proved my worth to the world. Saying I am ego-driven may be correct, but it is not about bragging, it is about showing "them" I can overcome.

It is about letting the world know I found a way out.

If you are a balanced, normal individual who prefers not to take risks, then you can put this book down now. If my story has resonance for you, then maybe the futures game is for you. Read on!

How This Book Is Organized

This book is organized into three parts. First, before you can do anything online, you have to get set up. Five basic components are necessary:

1. *Hardware.* A computer, monitor, printer, modem, and any other bells and whistles you feel are necessary.
2. *Software.* Charting, system testing, money management, spreadsheets, and so on.
3. *Data feed.* Some way of receiving data in a timely enough fashion to suit your trading frequency. It should be compatible with the software systems you are using.
4. *Online broker.* Browser or software based, whatever suits your needs. More importantly, the broker will provide you with timely fills (and confirmations), and a slew of useful online resources to boot.
5. *Other online resources.* Tools such as news, fundamental data, contract information, educational material, chat rooms, and message boards to assist you in finding good trades.

Picking the proper items in these five categories is the focus of Part One of this book. Of course, once you start trading, you'll want to update and adapt your technological and informational base. You'll be constantly adapting the way you scour the Internet for information and resources; you'll change brokers once in a while if you see a better deal, or if you're not happy with the service, or if you need more value-added resources on the site; you may at some point decide to change your datafeed, update your software, or upgrade your hardware. In short, your trading system will evolve, but you need all those elements to get things rolling.

Part Two is the meat and potatoes of the thing. The fact is, all the technology in the world isn't going to make you a successful trader. The key is how you use the information that you access. So Chapters 4 through 10 are about using and trading off of fundamental information. The fact is that now there is so much information out there, you must learn to harness it, streamline it, and analyze it to make it work for you. Imagine trying to wrap your brain around everything on the Internet! It is just too much. So you need to intelligently cull the vital bits from it to come up with a successful trading strategy. That is what Part Two is all about: building a system that works for you.

Knowing when to hold 'em and when to fold 'em is important, but it's not the whole shooting match. This is a game about money and not opinions. Each trade is a battle. You can win one or two, but if you don't plan how you will use your resources in the long term, you will certainly lose the war. From years in this business, I have learned that just as important as getting into good trades, is knowing how to manage your money. That is covered in Part Three along with some other closing ideas.

What Else Is There?

Trading futures has been how I have spent the better part of the past 30 years. The complexity of the game is where its beauty lies; there is just so much to learn. This book can only contain just so much of the wisdom I have gleaned in all my years. To give that wisdom its due, I skip over some of the basics and some of the more specific advanced topics. But please, as a reader and a trader, I hope that your education in the futures business continues. To help beginning traders get started, I have provided, in Appendix A, a primer on some basic concepts of futures. In Appendix B, I have included a select bibliography of some great learning resources. So many futures traders and educators have committed their wisdom to books over the past few decades, it would be a pity if newer traders thought they could get all they needed online. So keep reading. Keep learning.

Is Day Trading for You?

A final word before we launch into the nitty-gritty: This business of day trading is not for everyone. It may not be for you. What it has going for it is that you become your own boss, calling all the shots; you need no employees, and you don't have to knock on any doors to sell anyone anything.

You can trade from home in a bathrobe; you can call on a cell phone while fishing or backpacking, as I have done. I even stopped at a pay phone while running a marathon a few years ago to call in an order to my broker.

What I like best about the business is that there are no countless forms to fill out, no shipping, accounts payable or receivables, no inventory. I have no employee theft or rotten customers or whining employees bitching about their job or unwilling to do what needs to be done.

Indeed, this is the ideal business. Too bad it's so damn difficult!

It is difficult because there is a high degree of random activity in the markets and, on top of that, most people don't respond correctly.

For example, lawyers are usually very poor traders. Why? Because what they have done all their life, to earn a living, is argue, and they are good at it. So guess what they want to do with the market? You got it, they want to argue, to buck the all-important trend. That's a real wrong thing to do.

As one of my students (who went on to successfully run a $5 million hedge fund in London for a few of his buddies) put it, "Making money trading is like swimming in a river. You put your trunks on, grab a life preserver (our stop loss) then jump in and go which everway the river is flowing. You never, ever, try to swim upstream."

Other people can't day trade because they want to ponder their decisions, think and ruminate about them. Day trading is all about responding quickly. It is a business of the quick and the dead. If you are not quick, you will most assuredly be dead. Thus, you need to know how fast you can think—and act—when it comes to making decisions.

Still others are on the right track, but once they place a trade, they get carried away by the vagaries of their everyday business or life and simply forget to monitor the trade until it is too late, and lack of focus has caused a loss that they must swallow. Nothing more important than focus in this business; without total focus on the subject at hand you will lack clarity and the ability for a quick response.

The best traders I know have a unique ability to shake off their bad days and bad trades, they come back from problems and, do not get stuck in the past. If there is a common denominator, it is their sense of humor. They can and will laugh at anything, and in particular their worst trades. They have a past, but their past does not have them.

Is this business for you? No one really knows. I've seen brilliant guys and gals blow out trading while people who don't seem to have all the keys on their typewriter make a killing. One thing is for sure . . . until you do it . . . until you take the plunge, you will never know. But, since the odds are against you, I suggest you don't take a large initial risk and that you read my chapter on money management and paper trade for at least 30 days to find out if this is your cup of tea or cup of hemlock.

part one

pregame

chapter 1

what you need
to get started

Computers have become a necessary tool for every trader. The days of standard chart books have almost disappeared. Their static nature does not give today's sophisticated trader the flexibility necessary to make informed and researched decisions.

But what is necessary and what is just plain overkill when it comes to buying software and hardware? This greatly depends on you as a trader and the methods you will employ in your trading style. Trend followers and longer-term traders have little use for real-time quotes and sophisticated testing platforms. Day traders and short-term traders require the up-to-the-second pricing of the markets and will want to perform analysis beyond what is available for free on the Internet.

The Internet has made the world speed up and is an excellent first step for traders to explore before making their final decisions in both hardware and software. This chapter includes a list of sites that offer free charts and quotes. But before you get to this point, look at yourself as a trader and evaluate what it is you enjoy doing, as this is just as important. I know many individuals who make the ultimate jump from $80,000-a-year jobs to go out and become day traders. They follow every tick, and some love being tied to the computer all day and are learning excellent bladder control. Others find day trading too intense or difficult to master, and go back to their day jobs.

Type of Trader You Want to Be

Some self-examination is necessary before you make any final decisions about both software and hardware. Table 1.1 shows the components you will need, depending on the type of trader you are.

Hardware

On the hardware side, a computer is a must necessity. With the advent of faster chips and computers that cost less than $1,000, a good computer should be well within reach of any trader. Let's face it, if the purchase of a computer is going to strap you, then you probably don't have enough money to trade with anyway.

In general, the biggest and best computer you can afford is probably the right decision. Computers are getting cheaper every day and faster and faster. But software is also getting bigger and slower requiring the bigger computers. It is a never-ending vicious circle.

At the bare minimum as of the time of writing this book, a Pentium 300 with 32 megs of ram and a 4 gig hard drive should handle most tasks. If analysis software is in the picture, then a 450 or better is recommended, and pump your ram up to 64 megs. The advent of better internal memory handling in the computer makes it of greater importance to have more memory than a faster processor at this level.

I must also note that due to the lack of Macintosh software applications for technical analysis I'm leaving out their specs. If an Internet solution that is browser based is all you need, however, you could use a Macintosh. The IBM-compatible side, for now seems to have the lock on the programs we use, so no further mentions will be made of Macintosh computers.

Table 1.1   Tools necessary for trading

Trader Type	Computer	Back-Testing Software	Real-Time Feed	End-of-Day Data
Long term	Not required*	Not required*	No	Yes
Short term	Yes	Yes	Not required*	Yes
Day trader	Yes	Yes	Yes	Yes

* Recommended but not required.

Internet Connection

The Internet is becoming a large part of how we trade the markets. Now we can get data as well as all types of research transmitted through it. The more we rely on it, the faster our connection to it must be as well as the modems that connect. When using the Internet over standard phone lines, you should have at least a 56.6k modem. I won't go into the details of what the numbers mean but in general the bigger the number, the more data can be pumped through it and at a faster rate. Some areas are now offering digital subscriber lines (DSL). These are faster connections to the Internet that require their own type of modem. This modem is available through the company that sets up the DSL service. In addition to DSL, cable modems also may be available through your local cable company. The special modem required for this service is not yet available in computer stores, but it should be supplied by your cable company.

The main point is this: Since we are using the Internet more and more in our trading, it only makes sense to get a fast, reliable connection. This is especially true if you are using the Internet as a method of data transmission. If this is the case, a regular modem and dial-up connection is on the bottom of the scale. Look into the faster and more reliable connections offered by DSL, cable modems, ISDN or for you monster users, a T1. All these connections do require installing special hardware on standard computers, so there will be additional costs.

Monitor

Don't skimp on your monitor and video card. This may seem a little weird but since you will be looking at your monitor a whole heck of a lot, try and save your eyes any additional stress. A 17-inch monitor is sufficient, but if you can afford it go for a 21-inch screen. It makes seeing the whole picture a lot easier and allows you to step back to take it all in. I like to make this analogy between art and monitors. You don't look at fine art just a few inches away. You step back to try to take in the whole picture. The same can be said for a decent sized monitor. It allows you to step back to get a better picture.

The monitor is important but the video card, the part that supplies the picture to the monitor is often overlooked. Get one that has its own memory. This allows it to process images and charts faster and clearer. Cards come pretty much standard at 2–4 megs of memory so if you can get one with eight or more you are doing just fine. Also be sure the resolutions of the video card support a wide range. This usually indicates a better quality card with the higher resolutions being desirable. Resolution is the number of pixels that can be fit on the screen, and the higher the resolution, the better the quality of the image or chart.

Just as a final note on the hardware. If all you are doing is Web browsing, then a more modest computer will suit your needs. Remember there are thousands of configurations of computers out there. If you are confused at all, find a reputable consultant who can help you with your purchase. Try not to be oversold or undersold by a salesperson who works off commissions. There are plenty of sources on the Web where you can find great consumer information, and I recommend you check them out.

End of Day or Real-Time Data

Before getting into software, it is prudent to look at data feeds. The data feed you get will often determine the software compatible with it. So before you commit to any contract with a data feed, be sure your software needs will be met.

Data feeds come in many shapes and sizes. The main distinction is between real-time data and end of day data. There are also crossbreeds of these two but we will stick to these two categories first.

Real-time feeds provide you with up-to-the-tick information. When a trade is made in the pits, it is reported to the pit reporter and entered into the exchanges system, which then broadcasts it to all the feeds. They, in turn, transmit this to you and you see the transaction on your screen. Usually it takes just a microsecond to send the data out, but it can take varying lengths of time to get to your screen, depending on the transmission method used to send the quotes to you.

Transmission Method
This is one more piece to the puzzle for you to make a decision on. Here are the different methods of transmission available: satellite, cable, FM, and Internet.

I wish there was an easy way to rank the speed of these methods but there is not. It all depends on factors too numerous to go into. But I will try and simplify it as much as possible.

The standard, for a long while, to transmit data was through satellite. Recent advances in Internet speeds and modems have made the Internet the new standard. Satellite is still the best in most cases, but it requires additional costs for equipment and is not always available in all areas. If you live in a skyscraper or a planned community, it may not even be allowed.

Cable is often a viable solution for most people. Be aware though that the data is transmitted on sidebands along with TV programs similar to what you see when you watch CNBC. The ticker on the bottom is a sideband of data being displayed. Most cable companies insert local commercials into their programming. This can cause interruptions in your feed whenever there is a commercial. I have experienced this myself on CNBC. My solution was to choose another channel that was commercial free such as QVC, AMC, or TNT. Be sure you know what channels are supported by the vendor to see if they are available on your cable system.

My only real caution is to avoid FM transmission. It is the slowest of all methods and has been phased out by almost all the vendors. The delays in this method of transmission can be up to minutes from the time of the actual quote. This method of transmission is totally unacceptable for real-time trading.

So you have decided to go real-time with your feed. We have included all the contact information for many different types of data feeds. There are some questions you are going to have to ask and some determinations you must make before you call for information on a feed. The first should be which of the preceding formats you will use to receive data based on what is available in your area. Be aware that most vendors will try and get you into a one-year contract at least. Going real-time is a big commitment in both your time and money, so it is very important to use due diligence when making this decision.

When you choose a transmission other than the Internet, there may be additional charges for equipment ranging from the satellite dish to the receiver box. Some add a separate charge for the equipment and some include it in your monthly payment.

On the subject of monthly payments, there are expenses called pass-through costs or exchange fees, that the exchanges charge for use of their real-time data. These costs are above and beyond what the data feeds charge for their services. The fees are collected by the data vendor and usually are not quoted in the cost of the feed. This is a cost that cannot be avoided and represents a large source of income for the exchanges. These exchange fees can vary from exchange to exchange as shown in the following list:

Monthly Exchange Fees

Chicago Board of Trade	$60.00
Kansas City Board of Trade	$24.50
Midamerican Exchange	$7.50
New York Board of Trade	$88.00
Chicago Mercantile Exchange	$55.00
New York Mercantile Exchange	$55.00
Commodity Exchange	$55.00

There is a way to get around exchange fees. The exchanges make a distinction between real-time and delayed. Delayed data is the same data as real-time except it is rebroadcast between 10 to 15 minutes later. The amount of the delay varies from exchange to exchange. So if you do not need up-to-the-tick data and can get away with delayed, you can save yourself a lot of money. Delayed data is fine for individuals who want to get an idea of what the market is doing during the day but who are not doing day trading.

There is another type of data vendor, the end of day providers. These are mixed in the preceding list of vendors. End of day data is sufficient for all longer term traders and even for shorter term traders looking at a one- to three-day outlook. These are considerably cheaper than delayed or real-time data and offer all the information you need. Again with the end of day providers, there are differences.

Market data comes in many different formats. The most popular end of day formats are CSI, Metastock, and Ascii. When you get a vendor, be sure you are getting the data in a format that is readable by the software application you want to use. Try to avoid a vendor that restricts the use of the data in other applications or disables the use of the data after you stop your subscription. You have paid for that data and have the right to use it any way you like as long as you stay within your End User License Agreement. This basically says that you are not going to resell the data.

Also avoid scenarios where you have to download in one format and then convert and use in another format. This additional manual step can take a lot of time and this stuff should be easy.

As a last note on data formats, avoid Ascii format if possible. This is a slow way of accessing the data and will require you to manually enter additional information about that data when you want to use it. The nice thing about the CSI and Metastock formats is that all information about the instrument you are charting is also in the file. So when you go to pull up a chart on the Treasury Bonds, it already knows that each tick is worth $31.25. This is not the case in Ascii, and it would require you to enter this information.

Many provide just end of day data for downloading. Some provide intraday data as well. This intraday data is usually provided at the end of the day and is used primarily for backtesting of strategies. Intraday data is also known as tick data. These can be very large files, as in the case of the S&P where there are tens of thousands of ticks every day. There is basically only one format of intraday data that is supported by most of the software. It is the Tick Data Inc. format. This format can be displayed by the software application but usually cannot be imported into the software's format. This is important to know, as this data cannot be appended to the data you collect from your data feed.

Software Package

A distinction must be made about real-time vendors. The most popular software out there collects data from the data feed. When ticks are sent, the servers of these applications are responsible for saving and storing this data. So think of a data vendor being like a radio station. It sends out music and you listen to it. But let's say you want to go back and listen to the song just played. The only way to do this would be to record the song from the radio. This is how most software applications work. They must collect the data all the time during the market day, or when you want to go back and look at the data again, it won't be there. So if you shut down your software during the day and then come back later, there will be no data collected and you will have gaps in your data.

Better options are now available. Now the feeds are storing the data on their servers, and when you request a chart, they send all the data to you. Commodity Quote Graphics (CQG) has been one of the best in this type of technology for years. They are well known for having the cleanest and best data and extremely fast transmission methods. However, they are not compatible with any other software applications. So they provide their own front end for viewing data and doing analysis. This can be a great solution for those who are not looking to do system development and are more concerned with clean accurate data. At the time of writing, CQG did not have a system backtester in its application, but one apparently is due out soon.

In the same category of server side data, you have eSignal as well. Just like CQG's output, the data will have no holes as eSignal sends all the data down the pipe when you request it. No local data storage is necessary. This is true of their own front end software; however, this functionality is not available for all the other software products they are compatible with. So even though the data provider has the feature, be sure to ask whether the software you choose supports it.

Genesis Financial Data not only is an end of day provider and a great source of historical daily and intraday data, but also has something called "downloadable snap quotes." This is the ability to download information right up to current time. This is not delayed: It is up-to-the-second information. The trick is you can only request the data every 10 minutes or so. The time varies, as it is set by the exchanges.

Snap quotes can be an economical way for people to get started doing some forms of day trading. If your method of day trading is looking at 15 minutes or greater bars, you can snap quotes every time a new bar is formed and make your trading decisions. You can always upgrade later to a real-time package if you feel it is necessary. I highly recommend this to traders who want to get their feet wet without the huge cost of a real-time feed.

The final consideration when choosing a data feed is what software is compatible with it. This goes for both real-time and end of day data providers. Again, you must look at yourself as a trader and decide where you want to go as a technician. All data providers will provide you with software for downloading and displaying the data. Some have more advanced charting than others and some have more advanced technical analysis. If all you want is to get quotes and see some basic charts, then there is really no need to get any additional software. The data feeds will always provide you with some form of viewing the data. If you plan on developing your own mechanical trading strategies, however, then you will have to look at applications designed for more technical analysis.

In the past, the vendors left the analysis up to software companies. So this meant you had get a front end piece of software even to view any type of chart. Now the data vendors are starting to provide more advanced software in addition to the data. This makes it a lot easier for the end user as it becomes one-stop shopping. Always check out what your data provider is giving you as software. In many cases, it is more than sufficient for the beginning trader.

I want to make a distinction here on software. There are end of day software applications that would, of course, relate to the end of day data providers. And there are real-time applications that hook up to the real-time data providers. By this time, you should know which way you are heading, either end of day or real-time.

All end of day software have charting capabilities and basic indicators. Some allow basic system testing and development and some only allow canned system testing. Reuters Metastock and Omega Research's Supercharts have been the two most popular in the end of day market. Both have proven track records among their loyal users. Both offer basic system development and indicator creation as well as a large library of standard indicators. Costs are comparable and it comes down to user preference when making a decision between these two. Supercharts may have a slight advantage with the add-on capabilities provided by their solution providers.

This can be a great benefit for those that have no intention of doing their own development. Solution providers are vendors of add-ons like systems or indicators. I'm sure you have all seen the ads in the popular magazines for systems. Well, to run these systems, you need one of Omega Research's applications. These add-ons come in all shapes and sizes, so if you know you want something on patterns or cycles or Elliot waves, there is a solution already out there for you.

TradeStation is an excellent product, and my hat goes off to Bill and Ralph Cruz for essentially revolutionizing the futures industry. The advent of their application, now in its seventh generation with TradeStation 2000i, has brought the average trader the tools that used to be only available for the institutional trader.

TradeStation allows you to develop, test, and then monitor in real time virtually any trading system you can invent. Its powerful language called Easy Language has created a cottage industry for the solution providers. With that said, let's get down to the nitty-gritty of why you should or shouldn't own an application like TradeStation.

It is all too common for us to want the biggest and the best only to find out that using it takes more time and energy than we are willing to put into it. All carpenters have tools. But because they have tools does not mean they can build a house. Many people rapidly get in way over their head because they go out and purchase all kinds of software and then realize they don't have enough money to trade with. It is wiser to start out within your means and then move up to the software that meets your needs. TradeStation is a great application, but it is a complicated one. In fact, most users only master about 20 percent of what the application can really do. It is on the higher end of the price scale, so be sure you need it before you make the purchase.

So how do you determine whether an application like Trade-Station is right for you? If you understand the basics of technical analysis and are starting to formulate your own concepts about the market and want to test them to see how profitable they would be, then by all means you are ready. You are ready to start to become a system developer. This is the next step in becoming a successful trader.

On the other hand, if you are not interested in doing any development, then TradeStation type applications are overkill for your needs. Look at Supercharts or Metastock or OmniTrader. Any of these would be fine. Since they all do some basic development of indicators and systems, they can start you on your way when you decide to go down that path. Their editors for creating analysis techniques are limited in their functionality and pretty basic, but at least they provide a start. When you max out what these can do, then you know it's time to upgrade.

Another application to think about on the end of day basis is one just released from Genesis Financial Data. They have branched out from being a data provider to also being a software developer. Their new application NavSys, short for System Navigator, is filling a void out there in the middle-of-the-road price range. It allows extensive system design and testing primarily from an end of day standpoint. You should look at NavSys if you want more than what Supercharts can offer but are not interested in the additional cost and real-time capabilities of its big brother TradeStation. It is truly a system design and testing platform. It is catered to the individual with a short-term 1–3 day outlook in mind.

Compatibility with Data Provider

We started this section by tying into the data feeds. Not only must we match the type of trading you are doing to the data feed (end of day or real-time), we also have to match the software to that feed. TradeStation, for example, supports many different real-time and end of day formats. The most popular feeds for TradeStation are Signal, Esignal, Bonneville, DTN, and PCQuote plus a few more. At the time of this writing, Omega Research had just acquired Window on Wall Street by Market Arts. This acquisition will now provide them with their own real-time feed and should make it easier for new users to have a turnkey type package. TradeStation can support all the transmission methods to suit just about anyone's needs.

Nirvana's OmniTrader and Reuters Metastock RT also support multiple feeds; just make sure you match your feed to your software. Again, these real-time applications do more extensive research and analysis than that available from the data providers.

There are virtually thousands of combinations of software, data, and computer setups. Take it one step at a time and try not to go too fast. You may be surprised to discover that not one application out there does everything you want it to do. Quite often, we find ourselves using multiple applications. This is not unlike a carpenter who has several saws. Each one serves its purpose and to finish building a house the carpenter will use all of them at one time or another. Find the software that accomplishes what you want; don't be afraid to choose software packages that do only one or two things you like. Most people have multiple applications. Each one does what it does the best, so we use the software for those features.

The following list includes Web sites with charting and basic analysis, but is in no way complete, as many sites offer these features. All you have to do is go to any search engine and put in some key words, for example, commodities, futures, charting, quotes. We have taken the time to review the sites for usability and amount of information and analysis provided. Most are lacking on analysis but can give you prices and basic charts. Some will even give you delayed quotes throughout the day and can support multiple time periods from intraday to daily. Don't forget to look at the exchange sites as well; they also offer quotes and charts.

Web Sites of Data Vendors

A-T Financial Information Inc.
www.atfi.com
212-608-3870
Real-Time/Delayed Service
Data Feed, Terminal, Internet
 Service, Pager/Handheld
History, Charts, Analytical Data

Uses their own software. Very stock oriented. Futures available only as an add-on to the stock packages.

American Agricultural Comm.
 Systems Inc.
www.acres.fb.com
800-826-8145
Real-Time Service

Provides equipment. Commodities only.

BMI
www.bmiquotes.com
800-255-7374
Real-Time/Delayed Service
Data Feed, Terminal, Internet
 Service
End of Day/Snapshot Data, Charts,
 Analytical Data

Compatible with many analytical software packages.

Bloomberg Inc.
www.bloomberg.com
212-318-2000
Real-Time/Delayed Service

Requires their own terminal and software. Not compatible with other software.

Bridge CRB
www.crbindex.com
800-621-5271
Real-Time Service
Internet Service
History, End of Day Data, Charts

CQG, Inc.
www.cqg.com
800-525-7082
Real-Time/Delayed Service
Volume Analysis
Data Feed, Terminal
History, Charts, Analytical Data

Requires their own software. Not compatible with other software packages.

CSI
www.csidata.com
800-274-4727
End of Day Data

Format works with most software packages.

CTS Financial Publishing
www.tradeworld2000.com
561-694-0960
Delayed Service
Internet Service

Commodity Info. Services Co.
 (CISCO)
www.cisco-futures.com
312-922-3661
800-800-7227
CME Volume Analysis

DSC Datalink Systems Corp.
www.datalink.net
408-367-1700
Pager/Handheld Alerts

Data Broadcasting Corporation (eSignal)
www.dbc.com
800-367-4670
Real-Time/Delayed Service
Internet Service
Terminal, Handheld
History, End of Day/Snapshot Data, Charts, Analytical Data

Own software and is compatible with many software vendors.

Data Transmissions Network (DTN)
www.dtn.com
800-485-4000
402-255-3750 (fax)
support@dtn.com
AOL: DTNcorp
CompuServe: 72420,2114
Real-Time/Delayed Service

Own equipment and software. Compatible with other software vendors.

FutureLink
www.futurelinkns.com
800-553-2910
319-277-1278
Delayed Service

Own software only.

FutureSource
www.futuresource.com
800-621-2628
Real-Time Service

Powerful front end software provided. Compatible with the popular software vendors.

Genesis Financial Data Services
www.gfds.com
800-808-3282
Real-Time Service
Internet Service
History, End of Day Data
Trading Software

Provide their own front end. Data formats compatible with all the popular software vendors.

Investools, Inc.
650-482-3050
Delayed Service
Internet Service

Interquote (Paragon Software)
www.interquote.com
414-697-7770
Real-Time/Delayed Service

Jones Financial Network
www.pctrader.com
775-831-2200
Real-Time Service
Internet Service

LFG, LLC.
www.futuresonline.com
312-993-2239
Real-Time/Delayed Service

Internet-based application. Quotes and order entry.

Logical Systems, Inc.
www.bigcharts.com
312-939-3022
Delayed Service
Internet Service
Internet-Based Java Applications

MOBEO, Inc.
www.docupro.com
800-828-0870 (sales)
301-951-1733 (service)
301-951-1731 (fax)
Wireless Pager Quotes and Alerts

MoneyLine Corp.
www.moneyline.com
212-966-9797
Real-Time/Delayed Service
Internet Service
Data feed
End of Day Data, Charts, Analytical
    Data

P.C. Quote, Inc.
www.pcquote.com
800-225-5657
Real-Time Service

Works with popular trading
software packages.

Price Charts.com
www.pricecharts.com
800-221-4352
Browser-Based Charting, End of Day
    Data

Prophet
www.prophetfinance.com
800-772-8040
Historical Data, Internet-Based
    Charts

Data available in formats
supported by major software
applications.

Quote.Com, Inc.
www.quote.com
888-786-8326
info@quote.com
Real-Time/Delayed Service
Internet Service
History, End of Day/Snapshot Data,
    Charts

Works with popular trading
software.

www.rtquotes.com
Real-Time/Delayed Service
Internet Service
Terminal
History, End of Day Data, Charts

Internet-based application
provided. Stock oriented.

Reuters, Ltd.
www.reuters.com
312-435-8500
Real-Time Service
Handheld Service

Own software available. Works
with other software as well.

Standard & Poor's ComStock
www.spcomstock.com
800-431-5019
Real-Time/Delayed Service
Internet Service
Data feed, Terminal, LAN Solution
History, End of Day Data, Charts,
    Analytical Data, News

Works with many software
packages.

Telekurs USA
www.tkusa.com
888-TELEKURS
Real-Time Service
Internet Service
Data Feed, Terminal
History, End of Day Data, Charts,
    Analytical Data

Telemet America, Inc.
www.taquote.com
800-368-2078
703-548-2042
703-739-0451 (fax)
Real-Time/Delayed Service
Data Feed, Terminal, Pager/Handheld
History, Snapshot Data, Charts,
    Analytical Data

Townsend Analytics
www.taltrade.com
312-621-0141
312-621-0487 (fax)
sales@taltrade.com
Real-Time Service

Provide their own software. Primarily stocks.

Track Data Corporation
www.tdc.com
212-943-4555
Real-Time Service
End of Day Data

Have their own software solutions and provide data in formats compatible with many of the popular software packages.

Trade Signal Corp., Ltd.
www.tradesignals.com
Ireland
353-21-876525
Real-Time/Delayed Service
Internet Service

Internet-based charting solution. Uses a Java application.

If you build a system that does not require data from any outside source, you may be able to survive with just the delayed charting/ quote services available for free in many places on the Web. Throw a rock in the virtual world and you will hit a site that has delayed charting and quotes. Some offer lots of studies; some are bare bones. With these services, it becomes a matter of preference.

Some of the more prominent ones are discussed next.

Quote.com
www.quote.com

Although not easy to navigate, the packages available from Quote.com make this a very valuable site. Their LiveCharts.com is some of the best free market info you can find on the Net. The analytics are a little skimpy (as they are with most online data providers), so you still have to turn to a product like TradeStation to customize your indicators.

The for-fee area of Quote.com comes at a number of different levels that rival eSignal and tend to be a bit cheaper. At the maximum level (which costs $79.95 plus exchange fees for real-time data), you get live, self-updating charts displaying tick-by-tick to quarterly bars, quote sheets with one-click links and customizable columns, time and sales data, and aggregate summary data.

At the time of this writing, Quote.com was being bought by Lycos, so their awful format may change to something a bit more user friendly. In the meantime, use them if you can get used to their interface.

Tradesignals
www.tradesignals.com

This site is more a trading strategy site than a charting site, but their continuously updated, Java-driven charting application is interesting and worth taking a look at (since it is free at the time of this writing). This is the same charting application that is offered by CBOT's MarketPlex site. You can overlay a number of studies including Gann Fans and Fibonacci series, and many others. You can also choose between bar, candlestick, or closed line. You can even flip the chart around. One nice feature is that the chart scrolls horizontally for as long as a contract remains available, and you can zoom in or out as you like. This eliminates compression problems if you are trying to look at a lot of data at once.

P.C. Quote
www.pcquote.com

This quote provider also has a very clean, useful futures site with lots of resources at your fingertips.

Market Resources, Inc.
www.barchart.com

Barchart.com is a fee-based, Internet charting service. If you want to access their charts of commodities, many of the exchanges license use of barchart.com, so you can do your custom charting through their sites.

Wall Street City
www.wallstreetcity.com

This site, mainly devoted to stock traders, gives produce futures charts as well. The site is stocks-oriented, so the offerings for the futures trader are limited.

Equis
www.equis.com

This site offers all of this Reuters company's wares, but you will also find some free delayed charts.

chapter 2

all about brokers

The Art of Selecting a Broker—Frank Words from the School of Hard Knocks

One thing for sure about this business of trading is "you gotta have a broker," but the problem is most brokers "have" their customers. Opening a brokerage account can be dangerous to your health, mental well-being, and pocketbook. I hope I can shed some light on what not to do as well as whom to avoid. Most brokerage firms are far more honest and regulated than their customers realize. They prefer to see their customers walk away winners, and most firm owners play it by the rule books.

But problems develop.

These can usually be categorized as (1) rogue brokers or (2) fraudulently run brokerage firms.

All action begins with a mind-set, a mental view of the future. For brokers and brokerage firm owners that's a pretty bleak view because they know full well that the vast majority of their customers will lose most if not all the money they put up for trading. Maybe even more than they put up. Over the years, I have been fortunate to know the presidents of many commodity brokerage firms, big and small; they have told me there are few winners in this game. One president said, "I've been in business 19 years and have seen only two people walk away big winners. Sure, some make a little here, some lose a little there, but mostly what I see are people losing their grubstakes . . . several times over."

Because of that, brokers have a calloused attitude toward clients. To open an account, you have to sign papers that usurp just about every legal right or recourse you might have, except in cases of outright fraud and chicanery. Frankly, I don't blame the brokers for tightening up the legal loopholes to the nth degree; no one likes to lose money and brokers know most clients will.

Most brokers abide by the rules, but stockbrokers especially have been caught bending and breaking them, seemingly throwing all caution and financial prudence to the winds. They usually do this by pumping up the price of a low-priced stock they have personal positions in, to unload to you what they or their close associates have acquired. Once the switch is made, down goes the stock, a neat transfer of wealth from your pocket to theirs. That's the bad news; the good news is these guys always, eventually get caught. The even worse news is, thanks to a bunch of bumbling regulators, there is precious little chance you will be made whole once the Commodity Futures Trading Commission (CFTC) or Securities and Exchange Commission (SEC) steps into the game. Might just as well write it off, get out of the negativity and continue moving forward in life. Say what they will, government agencies are not here to help you, but to help themselves.

The point is, don't fall for brokerage firm hypes, don't lend them money. The simplest way of bypassing this potential agony is to deal with the larger firms and or introducing brokers. In addition to looking your broker in the eye, look at the firm's balance sheet, or that of the firm the broker clears through.

I started out fresh in this business many years ago, so I do not want to penalize newcomers by telling you to not trade with firms that have been in business just a few months or years. But it is good advice unless there is a compelling reason, or you have deep personal knowledge of the situation, that warrants the risk of dealing with any new firm in any business.

By and large, you will find more trouble and sleight of hand going on in small, relatively new brokerage firms (offering low, low commissions or plenty of free reports) than in established large firms.

Rogue brokers are a problem for one reason—money, or the lack of it, tempts us all. Individual brokers make their living off the commissions generated in the accounts on their books. No commissions, no money at the end of the month. The worst time to listen to a broker is a few days before commission checks are cut for the month; that's when they are most apt to cajole or badger you to switch positions, overtrade, and the like. Hey, wake up, that's life, that's how it really is.

A general brokerage firm rule is an account should produce in commissions what its starting value is in any 12 months. Ponder that for a minute . . . not counting winners and losers . . . *most traders have to make over 100 percent on their account value just to cover commissions!*

In case you have not figured it out, them's bad odds, folks.

The only way we can beat this high vigorish is to trade less, not more; yet most day traders and short-termers do it the other way around. Indeed, numerous brokers have told me they love to open day trading accounts because they figure the account will do three times its starting value in commissions before the sheep has been sheared. Think of that: The great unwashed masses of day traders must make three times their bankroll to cover commissions, and after all that work they then have nothing for themselves. Do you see the importance of undertrading now and why money management is so critical?

A rogue broker not only will get you to overtrade, but may also suggest he or she can do a better job than you or your current adviser. Maybe, maybe not, but that's not the way I would bet it. Jake Bernstein tells of a trial he testified in where a client, on his own, had run $30,000 to about $300,000 in less than six months. The broker called the client and said he, the broker could do better than that. The customer, being new to art of trading and hopelessly inflicted with a bad case of good luck said, "Okay, you call the shots and let's really make some money." Within two months, the account went to zero on the rogue broker's calls.

Here is your lesson; either you or the broker must be in control of the account, two people cannot drive a car at the same time. If you have proof your broker can make money at it (i.e., actual account statements from other accounts she's traded), go for it. Without that documentation, run—don't walk—away from the opportunity.

If you decide to drive that car down these sharp turns and winding roads, do not listen to any backseat broker bantering. Tell them to shut up, that you only want to place orders with them; and if they continue calling you with trading advice, close out your account. Really, the sooner the better, before you lose your hard-earned shekels.

Individual brokers are notorious for bad-mouthing advisers, newsletters, and the like because they, secretly, wish they were the adviser and didn't have to make 10 cold calls a day to stay in business, opening up new accounts to replace the ones that got blown out. Young brokers in particular can paint some pretty rosy pictures of what they think they can do. But if they could do it, why would they have to hustle you?

It's also easy for a broker, or adviser, to tell you how dumb someone else's trading recommendation was (Monday morning quarterbacking). After all, it is easier to tear something down than build it up, another natural human trait. My point is the same Ronald Reagan made in nuclear arms negotiations; trust but verify.

No proof, no trading with you.

All the preceding is part of the reason online trading has become such a big business. The human contact has been eliminated, making it harder for brokers to get in your pocket or mind. The purpose of a broker in any business is to put two parties together so they can hammer out the details and price or cost of the transaction. A broker is not an adviser; hence online trading removes the chances of a broker interfering with your trades. That's a positive for us traders, but since I have developed lifelong friendships with my brokers, it's also something I'm sad to see fade into the sunset.

Hold on though . . . online trading has not changed human nature and repelled the evils of greed. Online brokers, advisers, and analysts will still be out there to intentionally take your money. Margin calls and business pressures can turn very good people into rogues who will concoct some scheme to take advantage of you to profit or cover their past sins.

Tomorrow's electronic rogues will be different people; the media will not be the same, but the message will be. You will see four redundant themes from these artists: the first is anyone can do it; the second is, it's easy; the third is, it takes very little money; and finally, not much, if any, risk is involved. That's the hustle that's worked in the past, so the pitchmen will probably keep using the successful pitch! Additionally, this crowd will not be able to prove their claims with real-time trading results or real-time results from followers of their approach.

So, things have not changed, nor will they ever, from when Adam Smith wrote *The Wealth of Nations* more than 200 years ago.

Choosing an online broker is one of the most important steps in getting ready to trade. You can always seek greener pastures, but for sure you'll want to find a broker you are happy with.

To understand what to look for, you need to understand how orders were placed in the past and how brokerage accounts were maintained; then we can see how we have reached the point of on-line order entry.

In the past, you would call your broker to place your order. He would take the order and relay it to a desk on the floor. A runner would then either run the order to the floor broker or would flash the order to him. The floor broker would then enter the pit to try to fill the order at the best available price (in the case of a market order). He would then reverse the process to confirm the fill: floor broker to runner, runner to desk, desk to broker, broker to you. Did you ever play that kid's game, Telephone? You know, the one where the leader whispers into one player's ear a sentence like, "Mike bought a new Mercedes." Each person whispers it into the ear of the person next to him or her. Finally, the last player says what he or she has heard and it comes out, "Spike a pot of crude Euphrates." Well, things were never that bad on the futures exchanges. They couldn't afford to be. One way they have avoided this problem in the past is by repeating your order back to you for confirmation before routing it on. That eliminated a lot of errors. As you can imagine, electronic order placement can make things even more reliable—and faster.

But the first systems to use online order placement essentially did what you do when you call your broker. Only they did it with a keyboard and a modem instead of a telephone message. Brokers would get orders via the computer and would route them as they would phone orders. But technology has advanced a bit since then.

There are a few bifurcations of the technology: (1) Exchange clearing members are licensing browser-based and/or software-based order entry systems; (2) they are linking their systems into the order routing systems of the exchanges or are sending the orders directly to handheld devices in the pits. There are pros and cons for all these systems.

Browser-based or software-based, that is the question. And the answer is: It depends. Software-based systems can be faster and more secure. They can also be more reliable if they do not work through your Internet Service Provider (ISP). What you give up by using one is significant, though. First, with a browser-based system, you can access your account from any terminal—even a hand-held device with Internet access. With a software-based system, you must use the terminal that has the software to place your order. Second, with a browser-based system, you can place or change orders over the telephone or otherwise, and your account will always stay up-to-date because all your account data—working orders, modifications, and so on—are resident on the server at your broker. A software-based system keeps that data on your hard drive. This doesn't mean you can't change an order over the phone that you placed with your computer. It just means that that order is no longer trackable using the system because the ticket number associated with the modification is not available on your hard drive.

Then there is the matter of where your order ends up. The fastest systems send your order directly to an electronic order matching system like Globex2 for the E-Mini S&P. In these fully automated markets, you can get fill confirmation in a matter of 2 seconds or so. This kind of response time makes contracts that are tradable over these electronic exchanges ideal for the online trader. Another great advantage to these contracts is that there are *no locals*. What do I mean? Since these are not open-outcry markets and all orders are matched on the system, nobody has the information advantage over the online trader. This is key. If you plan on focusing on these contracts, find a broker that has this direct-to-order-matching capacity (e.g., Interactive Brokers).

The next fastest type of system sends your order directly to a floor broker with a handheld device or an electronic order book.

Finally, there is the type of system that routes orders to the proper desk on the exchange floor. From there, they are run or flashed to the pits and executed.

What to Look for in an Online Broker

Obviously, quick fills and a hassle-free account are the things you will most be looking for in a broker. But the fact is, since most introducing brokers (IBs) are using the same few order entry systems, finding the right system is a relatively quick task. Even some

FCMs are licensing order entry systems from other FCMs. So if everyone is operating on the same few platforms, what sets one broker apart from the next? The answer is service.

First of all, when an IB deals with a clearing member firm, they are accepting the responsibility to service the customer. That means that whichever broker you use—whether it is an IB or an FCM—they are the ones you need to deal with when and if there is a problem. So you want to find a broker that is not only effective online, but one you feel comfortable working with in person.

Another facet of service is what your broker provides you with in the sense of online resources. This is what sets your broker apart from others on a day-to-day basis. When you open an account, what kind of real-time quotes service do you get? What kind of charting and technical studies? What kind of research? What kind of news? How clean and reliable is their site? Any other perks like audio from the S&P pits?

In Chapter 1, we covered some of the online resources available to the futures trader. One thing I stressed was streamlining your trading routine. Your broker should be the hub of that routine. Your broker's Web site should bring together and present in one easily navigable place a good percentage of the resources you will use during your trading day. Choosing the right online broker is the best way to streamline.

Rating the Brokers

To rate futures brokers, list every possible thing you might want from your online broker, weight each criterion on a scale from 1 to 10, develop a grading scale of 1 to 4 for each criterion, then grade each category. When you are done with this, multiply the grade by the weight of the category, then add all the weighted scores together for an overall rating. Table 2.1 shows a sample rating sheet.

Other Ways to Research a Broker

Besides doing all the legwork on the dozens of futures brokers out there, you can also go to sites that will help you find the right broker, or at least narrow your search. First, you can usually elicit a lot of responses on message boards if you ask which brokers people are

Table 2.1 Sample rating sheet

Criterion	Weight	Score	Weighted Score
Commission + fees (round turn)	10	4 1 if > $50 2 if < $50 3 if < $25 4 if < or = $15	40 40
Speed of fill, average (E-Mini S&P)	10	2 1 if > 1 minute 2 if < 1 minute 3 if < 30 seconds 4 if < 10 seconds	20
Speed of fill, average (grains)	5	2 1 if > 2 minutes 2 if < 2 minutes 3 if < 1 minute 4 if < 30 seconds	10
Charting	7	4 0 if no charting 2 if basic charting 4 if advanced charting w/studies	28
Research	3	3 0 = no research 1 = minimal 2 = avg. 3 = good 4 = great	9

using and which they have used. In particular, misc.invest.futures is a great forum for sounding out a broker. Also try the boards at Ino and Raging Bull. Besides that, you may want to check in with www.sonic.net/donaldj/futures1.html#Online. This is a privately compiled page, and some of the info is outdated, but it does give you some insight. One last ratings spot is with FuturesWeb at www.futuresweb.com/ratedbrokers/futures.html.

The Brokers

There are dozens (if not hundreds) of online brokers. I have listed 10 of the most visible and some of their policies and practices at the time of this writing. But due to several factors—the length of the product cycle of a book and the speed at which brokers change their looks, their offerings, their rates, and so on—much of what is listed is going to be out of date by the time you read this. Therefore, use the information as a starting point, but do not assume it is still valid. Do the legwork. And find out about other criteria that you are interested in.

These are not the only brokers out there; there may be some that are better, some that are not as good. After the in-depth listings, I have given some contact information for other brokers.

Altavest Worldwide Trading

Introducing broker (IB) or Futures Clearing Merchant (FCM)? If IB, who is clearing member?	IB to Linnco futures group (LFG).
How long in business as brokerage?	3 years.
How long in business as online brokerage?	3 years.
Is a browser used or does it require additional software? Which software?	LeoWEB software.
What is the account minimum?	$2,500.
Is there a separate account minimum or online accounts?	$10,000.
Commission per contract (market order)?	$15–$79 return (r/t) depending on account size and services.
Can you process spread orders online?	Yes.
Commission on spreads?	Same.
Extra commission for limit orders?	No.
Extra commission for market if touched (MIT) or stop orders?	No.
Additional fee for telephone orders?	No.
Automatic execution confirmation via e-mail? When?	Refreshes every few seconds.

Initial margin rates?

Account access? Mark to market?

Are real-time quotes available? How much?

Other fees?

Technical analysis tools?

Access to news, fundamental data, etc.?

Additional perks?

Exchange minimums.

Marked to market end-of-day.

Yes. $69/mo. plus exchange fees.

Free delayed quote charting w/technical studies.

Hightower research, LFG research, Altavest's proprietary TradeScope newsletter.

American Futures & Options, Inc.

Introducing broker (IB) or FCM? If IB, who is clearing member?

How long in business as brokerage?

How long in business as online brokerage?

Is a browser used or does it require additional software? Which software?

What is the account minimum?

Is there a separate account minimum for online accounts?

Commission per contract (market order)?

Can you process spread orders online?

Commission on spreads?

Extra commission for limit orders?

Extra commission for market if touched (MIT) or stop orders?

Additional fee for telephone orders?

Automatic execution? When?

Initial margin rates?

IB through Vision, Limited Partnership (LP).

1997.

1997.

IOXM System (Browser version and down-loadable).

$5,000.

$5,000.

$25–$30 return (r/t) including fees.

Yes.

No extra.

No.

No.

No.

Usually within seconds.

Exchange minimums (mostly).

Account access? Mark to market?	Yes. Open positions marked to market every 5 seconds.
Are real-time quotes available? How much?	Yes. $50/day free.
Other fees?	
Technical analysis tools?	Free delayed charting.
Access to news, fundamental data, etc.?	Free news service that combines a variety of sources.
Additional perks?	They do handle full service and managed accounts.

Cannon Trading/E-Futures.com

Introducing broker (IB) or FCM? If IB, who is clearing member?	IB through Linnco futures group (LFG) and AlarOnline.
How long in business as brokerage?	Since 1988.
How long in business as online brokerage?	Since 1996.
Is a browser used or does it require additional software? Which software?	Downloadable and Web-based.
What is the account minimum?	$3,000.
Is there a separate account minimum for online accounts?	$5,000.
Commission per contract (market order)?	$22 return (r/t) plus fees.
Can you process spread orders online?	Yes.
Commission on spreads?	No extra.
Extra commission for limit orders?	No.
Extra commission for market if touched (MIT) or stop orders or other contingent orders?	No.
Additional fee for telephone orders?	No.
Automatic execution confirmation? When?	Yes, within a few seconds for most markets.
Initial margin rates?	Exchange minimums.
Account access? Mark to market?	Marked to market.

Are real-time quotes available? How much?	First month free, then 66/mo. plus exchange fees (through iTrade from LFG).
Other fees?	
Technical analysis tools?	Free delayed charting.
Access to news, fundamental data, etc.?	Market Voice—live audio broadcast from different pits (1 month free); Market Squawk—Live bid/ask from S&P and Bond markets; free daily research; free weekly newsletter.
Additional perks?	24-hour trading on S&P Mini; account status daily via e-mail.

Farr Financial Inc.

Introducing brokers (IB) or FCM? If IB, who is clearing member?	IB for Professional Market Brokerage Inc. (PMB).
How long in business as brokerage?	1995.
How long in business as online brokerage?	1998.
Is a browser used or does it require additional software? Which software?	Browser running PMBe.
What is the account minimum?	$2,000.
Is there a separate account minimum for online accounts?	$2,000.
Commission per contract (market order)?	$29 return (r/t) including fees; $18 r/t including fees if account balance is over $5,000.
Can you process spread orders online?	Not online. Customers must place spread orders over the phone.
Commission on spreads?	No extra.
Extra commission for limit orders?	No.
Extra commission for market if touched (MIT) or stop orders?	No.

Additional fee for telephone orders?	No.
Automatic execution confirmation? When?	Yes. Fills in 3–15 seconds for most markets. Orders go straight to floor.
Initial margin rates?	Depends on the customer (account balance, experience, etc.).
Account access? Mark to market?	Marked to market at end of day.
Are real-time quotes available? How much?	Free to customers on refresh basis.
Other fees?	
Technical analysis tools?	Proprietary interactive charting is in the works.
Access to news, fundamental data, etc.?	
Additional perks?	

First American Discount Group

Introducing brokers (IB) or FCM? If IB, who is clearing member?	FCM on Chicago Board of Trade (CBOT).
How long in business as brokerage?	1985.
How long in business as online brokerage?	1998.
Is a browser used or does it require additional software? Which software?	Browser.
What is the account minimum?	Depends on client and markets traded (c. $2,000).
Is there a separate account minimum for online accounts?	Same.
Commission per contract (market order)?	Varies depending on client's activity; $14 return (r/t) and up (including exchange and NFA fees).
Can you process spread orders online?	Yes.
Commission on spreads?	Same.
Extra commission for limit orders?	No.

Extra commission for market if touched (MIT) or stop orders?	No.
Additional fee for telephone orders?	No.
Automatic execution confirmation? When?	Yes. Auto-refresh around every 30 seconds. Can be refreshed more often to check.
Initial margin rates?	Almost always exchange minimums.
Account access? Mark to market?	Marked to market at end of day.
Are real-time quotes available? How much?	Unlimited refreshes; no streaming quotes as yet.
Other fees?	
Technical analysis tools?	Delayed charts w/studies.
Access to news, fundamental data, etc.?	
Additional perks?	Some brokers offer systems trading; T-Bills can provide 100 percent of margin; trade any market 24 hrs.

Infinity Brokerage Services

Introducing brokers (IB) or FCM? If IB, who is clearing member?	IB to Linnco futures group (LFG), LLC.
How long in business as brokerage?	6/95.
How long in business as online brokerage?	1995.
Is a browser used or does it require additional software? Which software?	Infinity Online (modified LeoWEB software) or Futures Online browser-based system.
What is the account minimum?	Depends on customer. Upward of $3,000.
Is there a separate account minimum for online accounts?	
Commission per contract (market order)?	$11 return (r/t) – $40 r/t plus NFA and exchange fees depending on client.

Can you process spread orders online?   Yes.

Commission on spreads?   Negotiable.

Extra commission for limit orders?   Yes.

Extra commission for market if touched (MIT) or stop?   No.

Additional fee for telephone orders?   Same.

Automatic execution confirmation? When?   Every few seconds, screen refreshes, checks for fills.

Initial margin rates?   Exchange minimums.

Account access? Mark to market?   Futures Online system marks to market intraday; LeoWEB doesn't.

Are real-time quotes available? How much?   Streaming quotes available through iTrade (for fee); free unlimited refreshes if using snapshot quotes.

Other fees?

Technical analysis tools?   Intraday 10-minute delayed charting from Trade Signals and Futuresource.

Access to news, fundamental data, etc.?   LFG's proprietary reports; news from a variety of sources.

Additional perks?

Ira Epstein & Company

Introducing brokers (IB) or FCM? If IB, who is clearing member?   IB to Rand.

How long in business as brokerage?   15 years.

How long in business as online brokerage?   6 years.

Is a browser used or does it require additional software? Which software?   Browser and software-based order entry.

What is the account minimum? $2,500.

Is there a separate account minimum for online accounts?   No.

Commission per contract (market order)?

$9.98 return (r/t) + exchange, NFA and other fees ($13–14 w/fees); discount for trades not held overnight.

Can you process spread orders online?

Yes.

Commission on spreads?

Same.

Extra commission for limit orders?

No.

Extra commission for market if touched (MIT) or stop orders?

No.

Additional fee for telephone orders?

Yes. Fee set by account.

Automatic execution confirmation? When?

Yes, usually within seconds. Confirmation is also sent automatically by phone.

Initial margin rates?

Generally exchange minimum.

Account access? Mark to market?

Full account access including account and ticket numbers on all fills; account balances marked to market.

Are real-time quotes available? How much?

Yes. $50/mo. free quotes; $.05/ea additional quote.

Other fees?

Technical analysis tools?

IraCharts are quite in-depth; lots of studies.

Access to news, fundamental data, etc.?

$19/mo. real-time news service from Bridge-source; trading pit commentaries.

Additional perks?

Free charting software; automatic phone confirmation of fills.

Jack Carl Futures

Introducing brokers (IB) or FCM? If IB, who is clearing member?

FCM.

How long in business as brokerage?

c. 50 years.

How long in business as online brokerage?

1997.

Is a browser used or does it require additional software? Which software?	Online, proprietary system: Jack Carl Electronic Trade Center (ETC).
What is the account minimum?	$5,000.
Is there a separate account minimum for online accounts?	No.
Commission per contract (market order)?	$17.98 day trade return (r/t) plus fees; $22.98 r/t plus fees.
Can you process spread orders online?	Yes.
Commission on spreads?	$39.98.
Extra commission for limit orders?	No.
Extra commission for market if touched (MIT) or stop orders?	No.
Additional fee for telephone orders?	No.
Automatic execution confirmation? When?	Need to refresh screen to see fills.
Initial margin rates?	Exchange minimum, generally.
Account access? Mark to market?	Account access through system. Marked to market at end of day; working on update.
Are real-time quotes available? How much?	Free real-time quotes on 15 futures; not streaming, unlimited refreshes.
Other fees?	
Technical analysis tools?	Delayed charting.
Access to news, fundamental data, etc.?	News, research.
Additional perks?	Access to principal exchanges around the world.

Lind-Waldock

Introducing brokers (IB) or FCM? If IB, who is clearing member?	FCM .
How long in business as brokerage?	1965.
How long in business as online brokerage?	1993.

Is a browser used or does it require additional software? Which software?	Both. LindConnect and Lind Classic ("Old Blue").
What is the account minimum?	$5,000.
Is there a separate account minimum for online accounts?	No.
Commission per contract (market order)?	$19–$29 return (r/t) online (depends on commodity) plus exchange and NFA fees; E-Mini $22 plus fees.
Can you process spread orders online?	Yes.
Commission on spreads?	Same as 2 market orders w/discount on intramarket spreads.
Extra commission for limit orders?	No.
Extra commission for market if touched (MIT) or stop orders?	No.
Additional fee for telephone orders?	No.
Automatic execution confirmation? When?	Yes. Software checks for fills every 60 seconds. Also, Check for Fills" button can be used more often.
Initial margin rates?	Sometimes higher than exchange-set margins.
Account access? Mark to market?	Online account access includes positions, account balance marked to market, order status, fills, working orders.
Are real-time quotes available? How much?	500 free refreshes/mo. in up to 40 commodities; additional $.05/ea.
Other fees?	
Technical analysis tools?	3 chart packages ranging from free to $15/mo.
Access to news, fundamental data, etc.?	3 news packages ranging from free to $10/mo.; 3 weather packages ranging from free to $25/mo.; Squak Box audio and video online of S&P pit.

Additional perks?	Portfolio ticker, simulated trading, twice daily analysis in both futures and options markets, systems trading, free subscription to *Futures* and newsletters; T-bills ($10k min) to meet margin; 24-hour operations.

Trade Center

Introducing brokers (IB) or FCM? If IB, who is clearing member?	IB to Linnco futures group (FG), LLC.
How long in business as brokerage?	6/94.
What instruments traded?	f/o.
Is a browser used or does it require additional software? Which software?	Must download LeoWEB software.
What is the account minimum?	Not fixed. Minimum around $5,000.
Is there a separate account minimum for online accounts?	Higher than regular, but not fixed. Around $10,000.
Commission per contract (market order)?	$19 return (r/t); $39 for system monitoring.
Can you process spread orders online?	Yes.
Commission on spreads?	Same.
Extra commission for limit orders?	No.
Extra commission for market if touched (MIT) or stop?	No.
Additional fee for telephone orders?	$25 r/t.
Automatic execution confirmation? When?	Every few seconds, screen refreshes, checks for fills.
Initial margin rates?	Generally exchange minimums.
Account access? Mark to market?	Nightly e-mail with all account activity.
Are real-time quotes available? How much?	Streaming quotes available through iTrade (for fee).
Other fees?	

Technical analysis tools?

Access to news, fundamental data, etc.?

Additional perks?

Customizable Java charts (delayed), technical analysis tips.

LFG's proprietary reports, live broadcast from floor.

Very TradeStation-friendly including technical assistance and on-line EasyLanguage primer; they do system monitoring; access to overseas markets.

The following list of brokers is compiled from the many brokers that are out there and is certainly not all-inclusive. Before making any choices, you should do your own interviewing and screening of any prospective brokers to make sure that you are comfortable with them and that they offer all the services you want at the right prices.

Alaron Trading Corporation
822 West Washington Boulevard
Chicago, IL 60607
800-275-8844
fax: 312-733-3912
e-mail: info@alaron.com

Allendale Inc.
4506 Prime Parkway
McHenry, IL 60050
815-363-5500
800-551-4626
fax: 815-363-5511
e-mail: service@allendale-inc.com

ALTAVEST Worldwide Trading, Inc.
27126-B Paseo Espada,
  Suite 725
San Juan Capistrano, CA 92675
949-488-0545
800-994-9566
fax: 949-488-7625

Angus Jackson Inc.
2400 East Commercial Boulevard,
  Suite 814
Fort Lauderdale, FL 33308-4030
954-772-1166
800-899-1166
fax: 954-938-8626
e-mail: info@angusjackson.com

Astor Financial Incorporated
Corporate Office
208 South LaSalle, Suite 1600
Chicago, IL 60604
312-332-0888
fax: 312-332-4880
e-mail: Info@limitup.com
www.limitup.com

Beddows Commodities, Inc.
725 North A1A, Suite E-202
Jupiter, FL 33477
561-744-0900
800-409-0088
fax: 561-744-5871
tradertcb@aol.com
www.bcifutures.com

BEST Direct
30 South Wacker, Suite 2020
Chicago, IL 60606
312-648-3871
800-759-0062
fax: 312-648-3950
e-mail: info@bestonlinetrading.com
www.pfgbest.com

Cannon Trading Co. Inc.
9301 Wilshire Boulevard, Suite 614
Beverly Hills, CA 90210
310-859-9572
800-454-9572
fax: 310-859-0547

Capitol Commodity Services, Inc.
8900 Keystone Crossing, Suite 1060
Indianapolis, IN 46240
317-848-8050
800-876-8050
fax: 317-848-8060
www.ccstrade.com

Columbia Asset Management
One World Trade Center
121 SW Salmon, #1100
Portland, OR 97204
503-471-1300
800-435-9444
www.usafutures.com

Commodity Central, Inc.
4802 East Ray Road PMB 23-268
Phoenix, AZ 85044
480-704-1982
888-59-TRADE (87233)
fax: 480-704-1985

Crown Futures Corporation
607 West Broadway
Fairfield, IA 52556
515-472-9833
800-634-9650

DEC FUTURES
800 NBC Center
Lincoln, NE 68508
402-476-7700
800-999-6587
fax: 402-476-8484

DH Financial
100 East Walton, Suite 200
Chicago, IL 60611
312-867-8700
800-331-1250

Eagle Market Makers
141 West Jackson, Suite 1201-A
Chicago, IL 60604
800-341-0834

efutures.com
One Insight Drive
P.O. Box 25
Platteville,WI 53818-0025
608-348-5980
800-437-7751
fax: 608-348-5986

Excel Trading Group
175 West Jackson, Suite A645
Chicago, IL 60604
312-461-9350
fax: 312-461-9370
e-mail comments about this Web
    site to webmaster@xltrading.com

Field Financial Group
1483 Chain Bridge Road, Suite 301
McLean, VA 22101
800-800-6304

First Pacific Trading Group
23166 Los Alisos Boulevard,
    Suite 242
Mission Viejo, CA 92691
800-748-6123
800-748-5084
fax: 949-586-7838
e-mail: firstpacific@home.com

FOX Investments
141 West Jackson, Suite 1800A
Chicago, IL 60604-3076
800-621-0265
fax: 312-341-7556
e-mail: info@foxinvestments.com

Frontier Futures, Inc.
4000 River Ridge Drive NE
Cedar Rapids, IA 52402
Futures information 800-777-2438
Stocks information 800-278-6257
e-mail: request@ffutures.com

Gruntal & Co.
One Liberty Plaza
New York, NY 10006
212-820-8200
800-223-9058

Infinity Brokerage Services
208 South LaSalle Street, Suite 1420
Chicago, IL 60604
800-322-8559
e-mail: info@infinitybrokerage.com

NetFutures.com
150 South Wacker Drive, Suite 2350
Chicago IL, 60606
312-277-0051
888-44-WORTH
fax: 312-277-0150
e-mail: info@netfutures.com

R.J. O'Brien & Associates
555 West Jackson Boulevard
Chicago, IL 60661
312-408-4700
fax: 312-408-4166
e-mail: info@rjobrien.com

O'Conner & Co. LLC
401 S. LaSalle, Suite 1700
Chicago, IL 60605
312-322-4550
fax: 312-341-8726

Rand Financial Services
141 West Jackson, Suite 1950
Chicago, IL 60604
312-559-8800
800-842-RAND (7263)

Robbins Trading Company
Presidents Plaza
8700 West Bryn Mawr, Seventh Floor
South Tower
Chicago, IL 60631-3507
773-714-9000
800-453-4444
fax: 773-714-0900
e-mail: info@robbinstrading.com

Trade Center, Inc.
105 Crescent Bay Drive, Suite B
Laguna Beach, CA 92651
800-894-8194
fax: 949-376-2812
www.tradecenterinc.com

XPRESSTRADE, LLC
Chicago Mercantile Exchange Center
10 South Wacker Drive, Suite 2935
Chicago, IL 60606
800-947-6228
www.xpresstrade.com

chapter 3

internet resources

Once upon a time, information—price information, fundamental information—was scarce in the futures industry. And when you could get it, it was expensive, usually prohibiting access to the individual trader. With the advent of the Internet, all that has changed. I'm not going to give you a lot of hooey on that front. The media seems to be doing a good job of that already. I won't preach about the Internet revolution, the way it is changing the face of the world in general, not just financial services. While all this is true, I'm assuming that if you are reading this book, you are already convinced. You are probably already familiar with the Internet and its enormous potential.

Where once there was a shortage of information, today there is a glut. You used to pay out the ear for the stuff. Now most of it is free. Before, the lack of information kept traders from performing at their best. Now, too much information can slow you down. Traders trade. We make our money by getting in (and out) of the market, not by sitting around surfing site after site. With all the stuff you can find on the Web now, you can get bogged down in the research. I'm not saying you shouldn't research your trades, but if the feeling of not having covered all the material that is out there is keeping you from making good trades, you need to streamline.

In fact, every trader should streamline his or her routine. What do I mean? It is the process of sifting through the available sources of information, judging whether the general content is suitable for your trading needs as well as whether it is presented in an easy-to-use fashion and is not already being supplied to you by another source. If all these criteria are acceptable, then add the source to your ritual. Test it out. See if it is useful. If you have to pay for it, assess whether its usefulness is worth the cost. You don't want to saddle yourself with a whole lot of overhead before you even place the first trade—we've already got brokers' commissions to deal with.

Streamlining evolves over time, with the result being an efficient method of operation for your trading. For example, you might have bookmarked FuturesOnline (your broker), FutureSource (your provider of fundamental information), Ino (for intelligent market chat), and Quote.com (your real-time streaming quotes and charts). Do you need TradeSignals? Chances are, you don't. You've already got all the charting you need. What about getting rid of FutureSource if your broker licenses their news? How many market newsletters do you want to read? Which have been giving you the best leads? Maybe you are trying to build your own technical system and you want to use TradeStation. Is your quote vendor compatible?

The goal of constantly asking yourself all these questions is to develop a seamless flow of price and fundamental information so that you can focus on the business of trading. The key to eliminating the stress of information gathering is to separate the wheat from the chaff of your sources; find a few select sources that consistently provide you with top-notch usable information and stick with them. Of course, you should keep poking around for more potential sites that could be helpful, but don't get hung up in devouring every last morsel out there. It will drive you crazy.

This section acquaints you with some sites you may want to check out to see if they fit into your streamlined routine. Some are lists of links that you may want to look at in search of good sites. These are just suggestions. I have spent a lot of time surfing the Net. I have my favorites, the ones that work for me, but I've tried to provide a wide variety of sources.

The nature of the Internet is that it allows for dynamic updating of information. This is a great thing, but it makes it difficult for a static medium like a book to capture what is available; services rendered, pricing structures, format and layout, usefulness, and reliability are all things that can change overnight, so to develop your routine, you need to scout around and find what is best for you.

Besides being dynamic, the Internet is also different from books in that it is a "hyper" medium rather than a linear one. You can always jump around from section to section in a book, but it has essentially only one starting point and one ending point. This is not the case with the Internet. Information is presented in a more organic fashion that can be both a help and a hindrance to comprehension. In the best cases, the hyper medium puts everything you are looking for at your fingertips in a clear, intuitive fashion, while at its worst it can hide things from you, sometimes the most useful things. This aspect of the Internet makes it difficult to accurately describe any given site. The best thing to do is explore and find what is best for you.

Different Types of Sites

Many guides to online resources break down their listing into categories like "megasites," "research sites," and "day trading sites." On its face, this makes sense. But a basic problem with this type of categorization is that the Internet allows any given resource to seamlessly fill a number of uses. For example, you may get news and research from the same site. In addition, you find their message boards interesting, entertaining, and informative. What category, then, does the site go under? You must either select one category or list it in multiple places. By trying to categorize it, you are doing a disservice to the medium in which it was created—you are trying to make linear a resource that is hyper in nature. So how should the listings be ordered then? I have divided these listings into some categories (e.g., Data Vendors, Exchanges), but I have left the bulk of them to float freely. These listings are designed *to be read* from beginning to end. If something sparks your interest, check it out. Otherwise, keep going. Each entry has a brief description so that you can judge whether it may be something for you.

In general, there are many types of resources on the Web:

- *Lists of links.* This is one of the most typical items found on the Internet. Sometimes it seems as if they all just refer to each other and never to anything useful. But that is just when I am frustrated. Otherwise, they can be incredibly useful. There are two types: general and specific. Since this is a book on futures, I have noted good *futures*links.

- *News.* These sites provide a wide range of breaking news, both general and specific. I have tried to note only sites that provide news specific to the futures industry. But unlike links, this gets a little hazier because you never know what news will affect the particular contracts you happen to trade.

- *Quotes and data.* The same information can be repackaged in a million different ways from charts to tables to snapshot quotes at speeds ranging from real time to end of day. Price information is some of the most accessible information (it is on almost every futures site in one form or another), but choosing the site with the proper format for you is essential.

- *Exchanges.* These are very specific sites because their classification is defined by their source and not the information they provide. As such, they are listed in a group.

- *Chat and message.* The Internet has created a medium for people to form virtual communities to discuss topics of mutual interest. Traders have picked up on this and, as a result, many futures sites offer a virtual place for futures traders to talk about just about anything that is of importance to them—from what brokers they use to what contracts they trade and how they trade them. There is a lot of self-promotion and hype on these message boards and in these chat rooms, but depending on your profile, you may find some of them useful and interesting.

- *Fundamental sites.* These include government sites. I have grouped them roughly together because they tend to keep track of non-price-related data (e.g., crop information, international trade data, Commitment of Traders data).

- *Industry sites.* Some sites are focused on a particular industry rather than on futures in general. These sites tend to be for people who are not necessarily futures traders but are industry professionals. In these resources, you may find insight into the particular industry, and this may aid you in your trading.

- *Research and commentary.* These sites come in all shapes and sizes. Some focus on a few contracts in particular, others focus on a wide range. Some have a fee, others are free.

Some offer trade recommendations, others are more general. Find the ones that you trust and that are useful in your trading.

- *Systems.* Many sources will offer you their own proprietary systems. Use them at your own risk. Some are effective. Some are scams. Caveat emptor.

These are just a sample of the different types of sites that you will find. Some will fulfill one function exclusively, and some will fulfill many. The key is finding the ones that do well whatever they do, and using them as efficiently as possible in your trading routine.

Exchanges

Some of the most informative and useful sites for futures traders belong to the exchanges themselves. This is probably because the exchanges compete more fiercely than anyone else for your business. More so, even, than brokers. Once a broker has your account, changing it involves some difficulty. But you can trade a different contract whenever you want. Therefore, the more helpful and informative they can be, the more value they add, and the easier and more user-friendly they make trading on their exchange. Exchanges, in general, believe in the saying, "An educated customer is a better customer."

Chicago Board of Trade (CBOT)
www.cbot.com

The CBOT site features exchange news and information including history, overview, membership, hours of operation, and holiday schedule. Besides these basics, the site also has information about seminars that they run. Many of these require a tuition fee, but some are free and are held nationwide, usually to boost the interest in and understanding of a particular contract. As of this writing, they were planning to offer online tutorials.

A great feature to help you keep on top of the game is their Listservers; sign up to receive e-mail regarding particular topics of interest: calendars to get reminders of Last Trading Days, First Position Days, First Notice Days, Settlement Days; contract specs to stay on top of any changes; conversion factors sent in an Excel file of all CBOT Treasury futures; Agricultural Week in Review and Financial Week in Review; margin updates; and information on their order routing systems.

In their Market Information Department, you'll find a wealth of information on particular contracts:

- *Market commentaries.* Besides receiving the Week in Review by e-mail, you can also check midday and end-of-day reports. A nice feature is that these are available now in RealAudio, so you can multitask while listening to them. These concise reports are a great aid in digesting the why and wherefore of the daily market gyrations from both a fundamental and a technical perspective.

- *Printable calendars.* These help keep visual tabs on what is going on in the agricultural and financial markets, noting release dates of Commitment of Traders (COT) reports, census numbers, export numbers, and plenty more.

- *Datacards.* These are neat summaries of the fundamentals of the contracts traded on CBOT.

- *Economic/agricultural report summaries.* These help keep track of reports that influence both the agricultural and financial sectors such as USDA crop reports, PPI numbers, export sales, CPI numbers, retail sales, and many other indicators.

- *Statistical reports and databases.* These files, available in Excel format, contain exchange data relating to volume, open interest, and so on.

- *Statistical annual supplement.* Published in book format for the past 109 years, this information on the performance of each contract is now available on the Web.

This is just the tip of the iceberg as far as the offerings on this site go. Another great area of this site is the MarketPlex portion, which is full of statistical and other information:

- *Quotes and data.* Delayed quotes, settlement information, volume and open interest, time and sales data.

- *Charts and studies.* Access to CBOT's proprietary charts and to TradeSignals interactive Java charting.

- *CBOT and government reports.* Access to proprietary CBOT reports as well as links to pertinent government reports including USDA, CFTC, and foreign reports. Also, some university reports may prove useful.

- *Weather.* Easy links to pertinent forecasts and maps from USDA, Intellicast, universities, and the National Weather Service. This is a treasure trove for the fundamental trader.

Overall, the CBOT site design is clean and promotes easy, intuitive navigation. There is so much here, especially for the fundamental trader, that you've got to dig around. And what you will find is useful not only for the trader of CBOT contracts, but acts as a concentrated set of links for the futures trader, making it a good addition to your information gathering/trading routine.

Chicago Mercantile Exchange (CME)
www.cme.com

This site, although not nearly as well organized as CBOT's, is about as robust. Particularly strong in educational resources, they offer:

- *Simulated trading.* For a fee you can trade for up to 90 days using a simulated account. This can be a good way of getting your feet wet or testing a technical system without risking cold cash. The Merc uses AudiTrade as their simulated trading partner. Check out AudiTrade's listing here for more info.

- *Futures basics.* Plenty of information is provided on how the exchange works, who's who in the pits, and so on.

- *Learning opportunities.* This is a listing of available courses and seminars.

- *Hand signals.* Although not necessarily useful or important for most online traders, this is a great way to understand what is going on down on the floor.

- *Correspondence course.* For a fee, take an interactive course in futures basics.

Even in their products section, this site is generous with its educational material. They have a commitment to the idea that an educated trader is a more confident and more active trader. I happen to agree. For each product group, you will find plenty of information on the history, the contract, strategies for trading, and how to trade the markets. Besides these educational resources, they also offer a comprehensive databank with downloadable data, as well as exchange news.

Perhaps the most useful section of this site is the Traders' Corner. On a daily basis, it has plenty of agricultural and economic reports, weather, information, and links to reputable news sources. A great feature is the quote vendor directory. The poor organization of this section means that you've got to sort through the resources, but it is worth the time to find the bits that you can then bookmark and work into your streamlined routine.

MidAmerica Commodity Exchange (MidAm)
www.midam.com

Affiliated with the CBOT, MidAm trades many of the same markets as its big brother only in smaller contracts. Their site is also smaller. Despite their reduced offerings, the organization and compactness of the site make it somewhat useful for traders of MidAm contracts. Ten-minute delayed price quotes are available as is a goodly amount of volume/open interest information, and so on. Most of this stuff is available from other sources, so you probably won't use MidAm in a streamlined routine.

Coffee, Sugar, and Cocoa Exchange (CSCE)
www.csce.com

The offerings on this Web site are about as exceptional as the design. Which is to say, "not very." But the bare minimum is there including:

- Exchange news.
- Daily market reports including open, high, low, close, and settle, volume, and open interest.
- Margin rates.
- Contract specs.

- Historical price and volume/open interest data. This is available only in Lotus 1-2-3 format at the time of this writing.
- Customized charting with some technical studies.
- Review of market economics. This is a helpful introduction to the fundamentals for those just learning about the commodities traded on CSCE.
- Exchange history, also includes some interesting facts.

New York Mercantile Exchange (NYME)
www.nymex.com

This site has all the usual exchange site items including:

- Seminar schedule of industry events.
- Contract information including background, specs, price data, termination schedule, exchange margins.
- A useful set of links.

Otherwise, there is not much else that sets this site apart from the others. In fact, it is quite bare in comparison to some.

Minneapolis Grain Exchange (MGE)
www.mgex.com

The site of this smaller exchange is compact and functional. It has a decent amount of information on the few contracts that they trade, and they have a relationship with Market Information, Inc., that provides data and charts.

New York Cotton Exchange (NYCE)
www.nyce.com

The poor organization of this site is frustrating. However, once you figure out their frames layout, you will find some pretty functional information on their traded contracts, including custom charting from barchart.com.

Kansas City Board of Trade (KCBOT)
www.kcbot.com

The site provides exchange news, charts from barcharts.com, simulated trading from Auditrade, and a few other resources. Otherwise, not all that functional a site.

FutureCom
www.futurecom.org

This exchange is not up and running yet at the time of this writing, but it promises to be the next generation of futures exchange. Essentially an Electronic Communication Network (ECN) for futures, they plan to cut out the middlemen by matching bids and offers over the Internet. We'll see if they can fulfill their promise. They will begin with a cattle contract and move from there.

IndexTrade.com
www.indextrade.com

This exchange was just being launched at the time of this writing. It is a revolutionary idea, but wait to see what happens (and how legit it is). Essentially, this is an offshore company that is actually a gambling concern. You can open an account with your credit card and begin trading/gambling with as little as $100 down. How? They do it by reducing the tick size to $1. They trade mainly indices and cater to the short-term player. Check it out. You can play for free with virtual cash. Is it the future of futures? Or is it a scam? I am reserving judgment. Time will tell.

Resources

Futures Magazine
www.futuresmag.com

Don't let their front page fool you. This site, despite a pretty rough look, is one of the best resources on the Web for the futures traders. Besides access to some of the best articles and information in the industry, you can get a ton of online-only perks. You can download items related to past and present articles including systems spread sheets, code for Omega products, and data sets referred to in the articles. These downloads alone are a great value-added over the print edition (which in itself is a phenomenal resource). But you will also find a great list of links under "Other Futures and Options Sites." This page tends to have some dead links, but overall it is one of the most useful pages for futures traders. It gives you easy access to exchanges' Web sites worldwide, futures commission merchants', and introduces brokers' Web sites (which make finding the right broker much easier), quote and data vendors, educational sites, publishers' sites, trading system software (as well as other software) vendor sites, and much more. This is one of the most fruitful collections of links on the Web, so explore and you will be rewarded.

Technical Analysis of Stocks and Commodities
www.traders.com

The online version of this classic traders' tool is a bit watered down. At the time of this writing, it didn't really add much value to the trader's routine in terms of online offerings. Mainly it is just a teaser for the print edition. Excerpts are available, but you have to go out and buy the real thing to get the meat and potatoes. So don't spend too much time on the site. But I do recommend that you go there at least once to subscribe to the print version. It should be in the mailbox of every technical trader.

S.M.O.T.A.S.S.
www.smotass.net

This is the link page to end all link pages! Its has a truly ama-teur look and some of the links are dead, but this is truly a useful jumping-off point. Their smartass name stands for Successful Methodical Online Traders Accessing Speculative Sites. This is *the* place to come when looking for new resources to add to your arse-nal. Whether you are looking for new dynamic sites to add to your routine, a new message board to join, a new newsletter, a new *anything,* come here! Also, they've got a great summary table and chart of Commitment of Traders (COT) data.

Commodity Central.com
www.commoditycentral.com

This is a very clean site designed to be a hub to futures re-sources. It does the job well with good links. And, hey, they have me listed as a "guru"!

FuturesStuff
www.futuresstuff.com

The site has a concise list of links, thoughtfully done. And the Trading Products section is a riot. Among other things, you can find "lederhosen made specifically to be worn while trading the grains, softs, and some currencies." Who is this guy, the Phantom of the Pits?

Ino.com
www.ino.com

Billed as "The Web Center for Futures and Options," this site is a collection of Ino sites that offer a bit of everything: delayed news from Bridge, the exchanges, and other sources; delayed quotes and charts; and some excellent message boards. An interesting feature is their focus on "extreme futures," which are the big movers of the day. By the time you see them, it may already be too late to catch the trend. But check out what preceded them—in the news and on the charts. It is always a good exercise to try to understand a major price move. Also on Ino.com, you'll find that they offer a bunch of premium services including a proprietary trading system and advanced charting. They also sell a lot of non-Internet products (e.g., books and videos) at deeply discounted prices.

Bridge/Commodity Research Bureau
www.crbindex.com

Bridge/CRB is one of the biggest names in the futures information business, providing news and quotes in all markets. Bridge went about acquiring a number of companies a few years ago, the Commodity Research Bureau being one of them. CRB has been *the* source for fundamental information on commodities market for decades. Their CRB Yearbook (also published by John Wiley & Sons), an annual chock-full of fundamental data, is considered by many as the bible of the industry. That said, this site doesn't have that much to offer the trader: news that they can acquire elsewhere (Bridge licenses their products pretty aggressively, so you have a good chance of finding this stuff on, say, your broker's site.), price information that is also available elsewhere (and usually in an easier-to-use format), and other data, such as contract specs. This site mainly serves as a marketing tool for premium Bridge products. There is, however, Bridge Trader, an online periodical that focuses mainly on fundamentals, although it has some technical articles as well. It is a bimonthly, so it is more features-based than news-based; checking out some of the back issues could prove educational. In general, though, this site lacks value despite Bridge being a great company and truly dedicated to the futures trader.

FutureSource.com
www.futuresource.com

This is another Bridge company that focuses on the needs of the futures trader. A much more informative site than the CRB site, and more futures-oriented than the Bridge.com site, this is the best of Bridge's offerings for the futures trader. They provide news, quotes, and weather. As with most Bridge offerings, the content is heavily licensed, so you have a good chance of finding it in other places. If you are looking to streamline your trading routine, you may want to find a broker who offers these services in a repackaged manner that incorporates other tools as well. Even so, this site is worth checking out to see whether some of the premium products may be for you. In particular, check out FWN news, real-time futures and options news that is great for fundamental traders; a Daily Sentiment Index that is ideal for the contrarian (for contrarian strategies, check out Earl Hadady's *Contrary Opinion*, published by John Wiley & Sons in 2000); and Hightower News, a market review and daily research report. You have to pay for all these premium items, but depending on your style, it may be worth it. Also, the message boards might be something you are looking for; their participants tend to have pretty intelligent commentary.

Invest-O-Rama
www.investorama.com/futures.html

This is a list of links that is done in such a haphazard way, you may want to spend your time elsewhere. There are some good links, but the organization is just plain poor. For example, on the futures home page, they have a list that mixes brokers, data providers, indicator and system vendors, and software providers.

Futuresweb.com
www.futuresweb.com

This site is mainly a links list and a site for repackaged information. Their links are good, especially the news links which are organized nicely in a framed layout. The links are divided into well-defined categories, and each one has a description so you don't spend all your time chasing dumb sites.

Find Commodity Brokers Directory
www.findbrokers.com

A resource for finding the right broker, this site has individual broker profiles that can be useful when looking for a personal connection. The listings are not comprehensive, but serve the purpose. This site also has a list of links that are a bit messy, albeit useful.

Bloomberg
www.bloomberg.com

This comprehensive news site has quite good futures coverage. It is one of the world's leaders in financial information. For really pertinent futures commentary and insight, go to the Columns section.

Marketcenter
www.marketcenter.com

This is an ino.com site that offers repackaged Bridge news and summaries as well as exchange news.

Futures.net
www.futures.net

Billing itself as "the world's biggest and best community of futures traders," this site offers repackaged market analyses from a number of brokers. Also you'll find some original and repackaged feature articles. In aggregate, all this could be useful.

STAT Publishing
www.statpub.com

"Market Intelligence for the World's Specialty Crop Industries Since 1988." So goes the motto for this proprietary news service for traders, growers, and dealers of field peas, lentils, chickpeas, and other specialty grains. Interesting, but unless you are trading these specialty items, not worth stopping by.

Reuters
www.commods.reuters.com

This URL will get you right into the section of the Reuters site devoted to commodities. It is free with registration and serves up plenty of proprietary news items as well as weather and other information. For more general financial news, check out the main site at www. reuters.com.

CBSMarketwatch
cbs.marketwatch.com

Their proprietary intraday Futures Movers updates are worth checking out. Besides that, you can look up quotes, but the site is otherwise not very futures-friendly. A great source of general market news, though.

Asia One Business Center
www.asia1.com.sg

"News about Asia from Asia." Dig past the home page and find a great deal of futures news and commentaries from a global perspective.

Benson-Quinn Commodities, Inc.
www.bqci.com

A clearing member of KCBOT and MGE, Benson-Quinn offers review and commentary on the contracts traded on those exchanges—contracts for which such review and commentary is scarce (hence the listing).

SolomonSmithBarney
www.smithbarney.com

This big-time Wall Street firm has a committed futures research department, but only their monthly commentaries are available to nonclients. Short on freebies, you may want to look elsewhere.

Grants Pass Futures and Options
www.markethotline.com
www.futuresguide.com

These two sites, produced by Anne Burden, CTA, together offer basic charting—a Java applet that appears to be their own proprietary system—quotes, market reviews, and trading recommendations. Some basic news links, a commodity calendar link, and a glossary link make these sites functional for a small operation.

Cotview
www.cotview.com

This site offers in-depth, fundamental information for the cotton trader. For the casual cotton trader, the "short comment" will do fine. The rest of the site is mainly for mills and growers. But for the speculator, the short comment gives a good understanding of their concerns.

Cattle Today Online
www.cattletoday.com

This is an interesting addition for the livestock trader and totally dispensable for everyone else. This is mainly a newsletter for producers, but the market commentary is particularly insightful for fundamental traders.

Jake Bernstein on Futures
www.trade-futures.com

There is access to all sorts of information and products from this seasoned (no pun intended) futures pro. Particularly, Jake's Weekly Commodity Trading Newsletter is of interest. Since 1972, Jake has been serving futures traders with weekly trends, timing, cycles, and seasonals. He also puts out a great sentiment index for contrarians—and lots more.

Gerard Commodities
www.angelfire.com/biz/ivfmnews

On the whole, I have kept broker listings out of this section. But when I do mention them, it is not for their brokerage service, but for another resource that they provide the futures trader. At this writing, Gerard had just begun a study of the Uninformed Trader. Inspired by the movie *Trading Places* with Eddie Murphy, this is something along the lines of those competitions the *Wall Street Journal* does when they throw darts at stock tables and see how those selections do. It might be interesting to see how their "uninformed trader" does. Just thought you might be as curious as I am . . . Besides that, they also have an expensive newsletter that contains some interesting studies for the contrarian based on COT reports.

Defender Capital Management
www.defendercapital.com

Humorous—and sometimes pithy—market commentary from this Commodity Trading Advisor (CTA) could be just what the doctor ordered.

Futures Zone
www.profiletrader.com

Billed as "the alternative guide to futures trading," this site has a very clean design and offers free daily research, live commentary, and trading signals. Alternative to what? I don't know. But worth checking out.

First Look
www.1st-look.com

Produced by Duane Lowry, a pit trader with 17 years' experience in the industry, this site claims to have a jump on the news, specializing in grains. Decide for yourself whether he is indeed ahead of the game.

Progressive Farmer.com
www.progressivefarmer.com

Good in-depth agricultural news is targeted at farming families. It is an off-the-beaten path source of news.

Farms.com
www.farms.com

Farms.com at this writing has no real use for the trader, but watch out! This type of business-to-business site on the Web could change the way futures are traded.

Pro Farmer Online
www.profarmer.com

This is a for-fee agricultural information service. Clean site with breaking news.

Fimat USA
www.fimatusa.com

Here you can find technical and fundamental research from the futures brokerage arm of Societe Generale, one of France's largest banks.

Commodity Futures Trading Commission (CFTC)
www.cftc.com
Although you probably get your COT data through a repackaged source, this is where it originates. You'll also find plenty of other reports and information at this site. The CFTC was created in 1974 as an independent agency with the mandate to regulate the futures and options markets in the United States.

Intraday Dynamics
www.intraday.com
You'll have to pay for this day-trading resource, but what you'll get may well be worth it: daily intraday commentaries, fundamental reports, and lots of technical analyses.

Market Technicians Association (MTA)
www.mta.org
The MTA has been around for over a quarter of a century as an organization that promotes the exchange of technical ideas, research, and understanding. Their site has a great set of links for technical traders including links to sites of members such as luminaries John Bollinger and Ralph Acampora. MTA also offers a certification—the Charter Market Technician (CMT)—program. You need to join in order to achieve it, though.

Equity Analytics, Ltd.
www.e-analytics.com
This provider of research and analysis has an interesting archive for the futures trader that includes:

- An introduction to futures markets.
- Educational articles on exchange competition, settlement procedure, cost of carry, the Capital Asset Pricing Model as it relates to the futures markets, and more.
- A technical analysis resource center.

One negative is that it looks as if this site is no longer being updated.

National Futures Association (NFA)
www.nfa.futures.org

This is a self-regulating organization for the U.S. futures industry founded in 1982. Remarkably useless in general, this site does offer BASIC, the Background Affiliation Status Information Center, a system you can use to see if a potential broker or CTA has had any regulatory actions taken against it by the NFA, CFTC, or exchanges, whether they won or lost any arbitration cases, or had to pay or received reparations in a CFTC case.

Reality Based Trading
www.rb-trading.com

Bruce Babcock was one of the greats in this industry. A believer in trader education, he wrote many books and articles on futures. This site continues his legacy by posting archives of articles he wrote as well as a very good, hyperlinked piece called Commodity Futures Trading for Beginners. All of these are great for beginners and experienced traders alike. And they are all free. There are also plenty of products for purchase.

U.S. Department of Agriculture
www.usda.gov

There is plenty here for the futures trader, but, being a government site, don't expect good organization. You'll find the useful information repackaged for the futures trader in many other places, including on some of the exchange sites.

American Metal Market
www.amm.com

Although the subscription area of this site is expensive, there are plenty of free features for the speculator who focuses on these markets. You'll find great industry analysis and commentary, and an okay set of links for the metal markets.

Platt's
www.platts.com

Standard & Poor's venerable power, gas, metals, and petrochem data, news, and analysis service offers this site. Really the only free thin here is the news, though. Otherwise, you'll pay—and big.

McGraw-Hill Energy Online
www.mhenergy.com

Access to McGraw-Hill energy products is the main function of this site, but traders might find the energy headlines on the front page useful.

Department of Commerce
www.doc.gov

So much on this poorly organized site is useless to the futures trader, it may not be worth your time to dig around on it. This *is* the U.S. government we're talking about.

www.home.sprynet.com/~tradex/

This is the secondhand lot for the futures trader. You'll find just about anything.

part two
the show

chapter 4

volatility breakouts—the momentum breakthrough

Systems can be developed in many ways; I am presenting here some of the ways that I have used for my system. There are others, in fact, about as many ways to develop a system as there are traders. That's the rub: All these traders do not put their ideas into a tight approach and/or worse yet base their concepts on how things should be, rather than how things are.

For example, there are systems that rely on certain lines coming across a chart based on angles and astrology. Before you chase this or any other system to its logical conclusion, ask yourself, "Is there a valid reason why this basic concept would influence price activity?"

Systems that don't work are not usually the product of bad research, but the product of poor groundwork. Check the premise before you turn on the computer or bring out your charts for a weekend of studying. If the concept has no underlying valid logic, all you will be doing is learning how to predict the past—sadly, there's not much money to be made in this fashion.

Once you establish a valid premise, you will need to develop an entry point, a protective stop loss, and finally an exit strategy.

A good system will cover all these bases so no matter what the market does, you can answer the prevailing question: "What the heck should I do now?"

Stops are pretty easy to work with, I prefer a straight dollar risk stop as opposed to a chart point or some magic mumbo-jumbo line. To each his own, though.

For exit strategies, you might choose to exit at a predetermined profit point, so many dollars of profit. Or you might use a time point: After X days in the trade, blow it out. Finally, you could try a combination of the two.

For entries, I like to add a small amount of the prior day's range to today's open and buy there, or subtract for a sell. Once the trade is set up, I still like to see price move a little in the direction I'm about to wager on.

Momentum is one of the concepts that can bring us short-term and day trading profits. It is what Newton was talking about when he said an object once set in motion tends to stay in motion. So it is with stocks and commodities: Once price starts to move, it will most likely keep going in that direction. There are many ways to measure momentum. I will not delve into all of them, just the ones I have found to work, and the concepts I trade with. There are other approaches; anyone with a fertile mind should be able to go past where I have stopped.

I doubt that anyone fully understood how the markets work until the mid-1980s. Sure, we knew about trend; about overbought and oversold markets; about a few patterns, seasonal influences, fundamentals, and the like. But we really did not know what caused trend or, more correctly put, how it began and ended. We do now, and it is time for you to learn this fundamental truism of price structure and movement.

Trends are set in motion by what I call "explosions of price activity." Succinctly, if price, in one hour, day, week, month (pick your time frame for trend identification) has an explosive move up or down, the market will continue in that direction until there is an equal or greater explosive move in the opposite direction. This has come to be known as an expansion in volatility and is verbally captured by the phrase Doug Brie coined, "volatility breakout," based on my early 1980 work.

It gets down to this, price has an explosive breakout, up or down, from a center point. That is what sets or establishes the trend. Thus we have two problems; first, what do we mean by an explosive breakout (how much of an up or down move), and second, from what point do we measure this expansion in price?

Let's start with the beginning, what set of data should we use to measure the expansion?

Since my working thesis is that we need a very quick explosion of price change, I like to use daily range values—the difference between the day's high and close. This value shows how volatile the market has been each and every day. It is when this volatility increases out of recent proportion that trends change. Expansion can be measured on a shorter time frame by scaling down to hourly, quarter-hourly, or even 5-minute bars. Profitable trades can be identified in all these periods, but my examples (and most of the examples in this book) are on daily charts because that is my preferred trading style. Feel free to experiment in a time frame that is suited to your trading habits.

There are several ways of taking this measure. You might use the average range for the last X number of days, various swing points, and the like. By and large though, using just yesterday's range as my comparison of volatility works wonders. Let's say yesterday's range was 12 cents in Wheat. If today's range exceeds that range by some percentage, the trend probably changed, at least that is the way to wager. This would be a clear indication price has had a new impetus driving it in a direction, and price, like any object once set in motion, tends to stay in the direction of that motion.

It is really as simple as that, a pickup in range, substantially greater than yesterday's range implies a change in the current market direction.

That also leads to the second problem: From what point do we measure the expansive move, up or down? Most traders think we should measure from today's closing price. That is typical thinking; we usually compare price change from close to close. But it is not the correct answer. I will get to that in a moment, but first let's consider points from which to measure this expansion: we could use the close, the average price of the current day, or perhaps today's high for a buy or today's low for a sell.

Let's look at the very best results of several nonrelated commodities using a variety of points for measuring the explosion. Table 4.1 shows buying tomorrow at a percentage of today's range added to today's close. The data, listed in order, show the commodity, percentage of range, dollar profit, accuracy, and average profit per trade.

Table 4.1   Adding or subtracting to the close

Commodity	Percent Range of Buy/Sell Value	$ Profits	Number of Trades	Percent	Average Profit
Cattle	70/50	24,556	265/117	44	92
Bellies	70/50	352,044	1,285/2,817	45	124
Cotton	50/150	54,485	200/465	43	117
Coffee	70/50	145,346	88/178	49	816
Orange juice	70/50	129,720	906/2,028	44	63
Soybeans	70/50	164,287	1,277/2,998	47	55
British pound	70/50	228,631	981/2,358	41	96
Gold	190/70	64,740	289/717	40	90
Heating oil	50/130	66,397	182/418	43	158
Bonds	110/110	197,781	420/905	46	218
Standard & Poor's 500	100/190	85,350	133/330	40	258

In this table, I have even provided the best percentage of the previous *day's range to add to the close* for a buy and to subtract for a sell. In this, and all data shown, no stop was used and you were always long/short.

This table shows only the best percent volatility add-ons for buys and subtracts for sells; and again in the data for Table 4.1, we added the volatility factor or filter to the previous day's close. Using cattle as an example, if price rallied 70 percent of the previous day's range above the close, we bought and sold short at 50 percent of the day's range subtracted from the close.

Next, look at buying tomorrow at a percentage of yesterday's range added to yesterday's high or subtracting that same amount from yesterday's low for a sell signal (see Table 4.2).

Although this concept makes money, again on the best-fit basis, it does not do as well as adding or subtracting a value from the close. A simple way to compare the results is to determine the size of the average profit per trade. In the add-to-the-close method, it is $327 a trade and $313 for the add-to-the-high and subtract-from-the-low technique.

Table 4.2 Adding or subtracting to the high or low

Commodity	Percent Buy/Sell	$ Profits	Number of Trades	Percent	Average Profit
Cattle	70	17,012	191/456	41	37
Bellies	110	141,288	278/608	45	232
Cotton	90	46,945	150/357	42	131
Coffee	60	120,573	36/86	41	1,402
Orange juice	110	60,825	261/582	44	104
Soybeans	80	99,568	444/1,022	43	97
British pound	120	175,506	295/698	42	251
Gold	130	57,600	198/504	39	114
Heating oil	60	43,117	168/435	38	99
Bonds	90	154,968	290/605	47	256
Standard & Poor's 500	100	80,787	569/225	40	141

The next set of data adds a percentage of today's range to tomorrow's open and buys there for a long entry or subtracts a percentage of today's range from the opening for a sell. The results appear in Table 4.3.

A careful look at the data shows us the average profit per trade is higher at $389 and the accuracy is also higher; five commodities

Table 4.3 Adding or subtracting to tomorrow's open

Commodity	Percent Buy/Sell	$ Profits	Number of Trades	Percent +	Average Profit
Cattle	140	37,992	124/230	53	163
Bellies	70	303,792	1,076/2,236	48	135
Cotton	60	71,895	988/454	45	73
Coffee	130	135,915	38/63	60	2,157
Orange juice	50	169,140	1,184/2,754	52	75
Soybeans	100	228,293	620/1,293	47	176
British pound	130	242,062	300/600	50	403
Gold	130	95,070	290/634	45	149
Heating oil	140	42,163	87/196	44	215
Bonds	100	227,468	464/919	50	247
Standard & Poor's 500	50	247,850	768/1,727	44	143

in this test showed an accuracy of 50 percent or higher while none of them did in the first two tests.

My conclusion is that the best point to add or subtract a volatility expansion value to is tomorrow's open. I have always traded this technique with the open, but in preparation for this book, I did the preceding tests to see whether my judgment was right and was pleased to see facts fit my intuitive conclusion.

As short-term traders, we can use this concept to tell us there is a high probability of a further extension of price we can capitalize on. I will not trade *just because of such an entry,* but will use this as my entry technique when the time and conditions are correct.

Of all the trend entry approaches I know about, from moving averages to trendlines, oscillators to Ouija boards, and fancy math to simple charts; I have never seen a more consistently profitable mechanical entry technique than volatility breakouts. It is the most consistent of all entries I have ever traded, researched, or seen. Now let's look at some ways of using this basic concept.

Simple Daily Range Breakouts

From the preceding, we have learned that we should *add our breakout value to tomorrow's opening.* Now the questions begin; What's the best value? There are several good ones, but the simplest is to take today's range adding a portion of it to tomorrow's opening. Just that simple approach has been a consistent moneymaker since I first discovered it almost 20 years ago.

It is now time to go a bit beyond these results and create a trading model that is actually tradable (i.e., it makes money in an acceptable fashion). Figure 4.1 shows the result of buying and selling bonds on the open every day at a distance of 100 percent of the previous day's range above the open for a buy and 100 percent below the open for a sell.

A protective stop of $1,500 or 50 percent of the previous day's range subtracted from our entry is used as our protective stop while our exit is the bailout or the first profitable opening after entry technique. This does make money, $73,468 with 80 percent accuracy on 651 trades. On average, the system makes $7,000 a year and would require a $13,000 bankroll to net the 70 percent a year gain. The drawdown of only $10,031 is quite good for such a basic system. A problem can be seen in that the average profit per trade

Figure 4.1   A trading model that works

```
Data            : DAY T-BONDS        67/99
Calc Dates      : 01/01/90 - 08/25/98

Num. Conv. P. Value  Comm  Slippage  Margin  Format  Drive:\Path\FileName
-----------------------------------------------------------------------------
 144  -3  $  31.250  $  0  $     0   $ 3,000   CSI    C:\GD\BACK67\F061.DTA
```

//////////////////////////// ALL TRADES - Test 1 \\\\\\\\\\\\\\\\\\\\\\\\\\\

Total net profit	$73,468.75		
Gross profit	$213,156.25	Gross loss	-139,687.50
Total # of trades	651	Percent profitable	80%
Number winning trades	523	Number losing trades	128
Largest winning trade	$3,968.75	Largest losing trade	$-1,812.50
Average winning trade	$407.56	Average losing trade	$-1,091.31
Ratio avg win/avg loss	0.37	Avg trade (win & loss)	$112.86
Max consecutive winners	20	Max consecutive losers	4
Avg # bars in winners	1	Avg # bars in losers	2
Max closed-out drawdown	$-10,031.25	Max intra-day drawdown	$-10,031.25
Profit factor	1.52	Max # of contracts held	1
Account size required	$13,031.25	Return on account	563%

Figure 4.2   Trade day of the week: Monday

//////////////////////////// ALL TRADES - Test 5 \\\\\\\\\\\\\\\\\\\\\\\\\\\

Total net profit	$9,500.00	**Monday**	
Gross profit	$22,968.75	Gross loss	$-13,468.75
Total # of trades	77	Percent profitable	87%
Number winning trades	67	Number losing trades	10
Largest winning trade	$1,437.50	Largest losing trade	$-1,500.00
Average winning trade	$342.82	Average losing trade	$-1,346.87
Ratio avg win/avg loss	0.25	Avg trade (win & loss)	$123.38
Max consecutive winners	15	Max consecutive losers	1
Avg # bars in winners	1	Avg # bars in losers	4
Max closed-out drawdown	$-2,843.75	Max intra-day drawdown	$-2,968.75
Profit factor	1.70	Max # of contracts held	1
Account size required	$5,968.75	Return on account	159%

//////////////////////////// SHORT TRADES - Test 5 \\\\\\\\\\\\\\\\\\\\\\\\\\\

Total net profit	$5,218.75		
Gross profit	$11,656.25	Gross loss	$-6,437.50
Total # of trades	37	Percent profitable	86%
Number winning trades	32	Number losing trades	5
Largest winning trade	$1,437.50	Largest losing trade	$-1,500.00
Average winning trade	$364.26	Average losing trade	$-1,287.50
Ratio avg win/avg loss	0.28	Avg trade (win & loss)	$141.05
Max consecutive winners	15	Max consecutive losers	2
Avg # bars in winners	1	Avg # bars in losers	5
Max closed-out drawdown	$-3,406.25	Max intra-day drawdown	$-3,406.25
Profit factor	1.81	Max # of contracts held	1
Account size required	$6,406.25	Return on account	81%

is only $112.86; this needs to be higher. The data set is from 1990 through August 1998.

Any idea how we might accomplish such a lofty goal? For now, let's try our basic TDW (Trade Day of Week) strategy to see what happens if we only take buy and sells on certain specific days. To get a sense of this, Figures 4.2 through 4.6 show the buys for each day of the week, then the sells for each day, and finally we put together the best buy/sell days for a working model we can actually trade.

The listings indicate the best days to buy have been Tuesdays and Thursdays, whereas the best sell days have been Wednesdays and Thursdays. Figure 4.7 shows that if we restrict trading to just these days, we don't make as much money, only $56,437, but just about cut the number of trades in half and boost our profits up to

---

Figure 4.3   Trade day of the week: Tuesday

/////////////////////////// LONG TRADES - Test 1 \\\\\\\\\\\\\\\\\\\\\\\\\\\\\\\

		Tuesday	
Total net profit	$21,718.75		
Gross profit	$38,062.50	Gross loss	$-16,343.75
Total # of trades	108	Percent profitable	89%
Number winning trades	97	Number losing trades	11
Largest winning trade	$1,687.50	Largest losing trade	$-1,500.00
Average winning trade	$392.40	Average losing trade	$-1,485.80
Ratio avg win/avg loss	0.26	Avg trade (win & loss)	$201.10
Max consecutive winners	42	Max consecutive losers	2
Avg # bars in winners	1	Avg # bars in losers	2

/////////////////////////// SHORT TRADES - Test 1 \\\\\\\\\\\\\\\\\\\\\\\\\\\\\\\

Total net profit	$-6,375.00		
Gross profit	$21,625.00	Gross loss	$-28,000.00
Total # of trades	79	Percent profitable	75%
Number winning trades	60	Number losing trades	19
Largest winning trade	$1,437.50	Largest losing trade	$-1,687.50
Average winning trade	$360.42	Average losing trade	$-1,473.68
Ratio avg win/avg loss	0.24	Avg trade (win & loss)	$-80.70
Max consecutive winners	14	Max consecutive losers	3
Avg # bars in winners	1	Avg # bars in losers	4
Max closed-out drawdown	$-11,156.25	Max intra-day drawdown	$-11,593.75
Profit factor	0.77	Max # of contracts held	1
Account size required	$14,593.75	Return on account	-43%

Figure 4.4   Trade day of the week: Wednesday

```
/////////////////////////// LONG TRADES   - Test 2 \\\\\\\\\\\\\\\\\\\\\\\\\\\\
Total net profit          $5,218.75              Wednesday
Gross profit              $23,343.75  Gross loss              $-18,125.00

Total # of trades         77          Percent profitable      84%
Number winning trades     65          Number losing trades    12

Largest winning trade     $1,406.25   Largest losing trade    $-1,625.00
Average winning trade     $359.13     Average losing trade    $-1,510.42
Ratio avg win/avg loss    0.23        Avg trade (win & loss)  $67.78

Max consecutive winners   17          Max consecutive losers  2
Avg # bars in winners     1           Avg # bars in losers    2



/////////////////////////// SHORT TRADES  - Test 2 \\\\\\\\\\\\\\\\\\\\\\\\\\\\
Total net profit          $12,250.00
Gross profit              $27,500.00  Gross loss              $-15,250.00

Total # of trades         68          Percent profitable      85%
Number winning trades     58          Number losing trades    10

Largest winning trade     $1,562.50   Largest losing trade    $-1,718.75
Average winning trade     $474.14     Average losing trade    $-1,525.00
Ratio avg win/avg loss    0.31        Avg trade (win & loss)  $180.15

Max consecutive winners   14          Max consecutive losers  2
Avg # bars in winners     1           Avg # bars in losers    2

Max closed-out drawdown   $-3,000.00  Max intra-day drawdown  $-3,000.00
Profit factor             1.80        Max # of contracts held 1
Account size required     $6,000.00   Return on account       204%
```

$173 on average, a number worth trading for. Your lesson here is that the Trade Day of Week (TDW) can make a big difference in your system's performance. Best yet, the drawdown plummets to only $3,500 from $10,031 and the accuracy jumps to 84 percent. This is a big improvement, as explained in the discussion of money management in Chapter 12.

Most of my research has focused on TDW and TDM. For day traders, though, an equivalent study should be done to create a filter for intraday traders. The trading day has its own characteristics, and these can be broken down into more profitable Trading Hours of the Day (THD). This book can't give you all the answers, but it can show you how to find them on your own. The more you experiment, the more answers you will find. I've been doing trading for years, and I keep experimenting and learning.

Figure 4.5 Trade day of the week: Thursday

```
//////////////////////////// LONG TRADES  - Test 3 \\\\\\\\\\\\\\\\\\\\\\\\\\\\\\\
                                                          Thursday
Total net profit      $15,875.00
Gross profit          $32,562.50     Gross loss              $-16,687.50

Total # of trades             88     Percent profitable              87%
Number winning trades         77     Number losing trades            11

Largest winning trade  $1,687.50     Largest losing trade     $-1,687.50
Average winning trade    $422.89     Average losing trade     $-1,517.05
Ratio avg win/avg loss      0.27     Avg trade (win & loss)      $180.40

Max consecutive winners       17     Max consecutive losers           1
Avg # bars in winners          1     Avg # bars in losers             1
```

```
//////////////////////////// SHORT TRADES  - Test 3 \\\\\\\\\\\\\\\\\\\\\\\\\\\\\\\
Total net profit      $15,937.50
Gross profit          $33,937.50     Gross loss              $-18,000.00

Total # of trades             81     Percent profitable              85%
Number winning trades         69     Number losing trades            12

Largest winning trade  $2,406.25     Largest losing trade     $-1,500.00
Average winning trade    $491.85     Average losing trade     $-1,500.00
Ratio avg win/avg loss      0.32     Avg trade (win & loss)      $196.76

Max consecutive winners       13     Max consecutive losers           1
Avg # bars in winners          1     Avg # bars in losers             3

Max closed-out drawdown $-3,343.75   Max intra-day drawdown   $-3,937.50
Profit factor               1.88     Max # of contracts held          1
Account size required  $6,937.50     Return on account             229%
```

A Look at Volatility in the S&P 500

Does this concept have application for the S&P 500?

Although there can be no doubt about this technique working with a 50 percent volatility expansion, we can improve on it a great deal. How? By using something we already know about, the impact of TDW. The next set of data shows the volatility breakout performance by each day of the week for the S&P 500. The exit is the same as with the bonds shown earlier. Clearly, some days are better than others to trade. Figures 4.8 through 4.12 show the buy signals by day of week; Figures 4.13 through 4.17 show sell signals by day of week.

Figure 4.18 shows trading on just the more influential days. The best days to be a buyer were all days except Thursday and Friday, while the best sell day was Thursday, with Friday a push, but it is used in the following listing. This is not a bad system, it "made" $227,822 with 75 percent accuracy on 1,333 trades and had a very

Figure 4.6 Trade day of the week: Friday

```
///////////////////////////// LONG TRADES   - Test 4 \\\\\\\\\\\\\\\\\\\\\\\\\\\\
Total net profit          $7,250.00           Friday
Gross profit              $39,218.75   Gross loss                $-31,968.75

Total # of trades         117          Percent profitable        82%
Number winning trades     96           Number losing trades      21

Largest winning trade     $1,656.25    Largest losing trade      $-2,000.00
Average winning trade     $408.53      Average losing trade      $-1,522.32
Ratio avg win/avg loss    0.26         Avg trade (win & loss)    $61.97

Max consecutive winners   17           Max consecutive losers    2
Avg # bars in winners     2            Avg # bars in losers      2
```

```
///////////////////////////// SHORT TRADES  - Test 4 \\\\\\\\\\\\\\\\\\\\\\\\\\\\
Total net profit          $12,468.75
Gross profit              $35,906.25   Gross loss                $-23,437.50

Total # of trades         95           Percent profitable        82%
Number winning trades     78           Number losing trades      17

Largest winning trade     $3,968.75    Largest losing trade      $-1,531.25
Average winning trade     $460.34      Average losing trade      $-1,378.68
Ratio avg win/avg loss    0.33         Avg trade (win & loss)    $131.25

Max consecutive winners   12           Max consecutive losers    3
Avg # bars in winners     1            Avg # bars in losers      3

Max closed-out drawdown   $-4,093.75   Max intra-day drawdown    $-4,093.75
Profit factor             1.53         Max # of contracts held   1
Account size required     $7,093.75    Return on account         175%
```

small drawdown of only $13,737. I would prefer a larger average profit per trade than the $170 shown here.

An astute, thinking trader should be asking questions like, "Could we use a closer volatility expansion number to be a buyer on the more bullish days and a farther away entry value on the days that don't work so well with the 50 percent value? And how about our exit, would it pay off to hold longer on the more bullish/bearish days?"

These questions can continue indefinitely, but need to be asked to optimize performance. Proof that research pays off is offered by Figure 4.19, which shows the use of the preceding rules, except that the buy entry comes at 40 percent of the previous day's range added to the open, the sell entry at 200 percent of the range subtracted from the open. There is a big difference here; while it actually makes a little less money ($14,000), the accuracy goes to

Figure 4.7 Restricting trade days makes a big difference

```
Data           : DAY T-BONDS          67/99
Calc Dates     : 01/01/90 - 08/25/98

Num. Conv. P. Value  Comm  Slippage  Margin  Format  Drive:\Path\FileName
---------------------------------------------------------------------------
 144   -3  $ 31.250  $ 0   $ 0       $ 3,000  CSI    C:\GD\BACK67\F061.DTA
```

/////////////////////////// ALL TRADES - Test 1 \\\\\\\\\\\\\\\\\\\\\\\\\\\\\\

Total net profit	$56,437.50		
Gross profit	$122,375.00	Gross loss	$-65,937.50
Total # of trades	326	Percent profitable	84%
Number winning trades	277	Number losing trades	49
Largest winning trade	$2,406.25	Largest losing trade	$-1,718.75
Average winning trade	$441.79	Average losing trade	$-1,345.66
Ratio avg win/avg loss	0.32	Avg trade (win & loss)	$173.12
Max consecutive winners	23	Max consecutive losers	2
Avg # bars in winners	1	Avg # bars in losers	2
Max closed-out drawdown	$-3,500.00	Max intra-day drawdown	$-3,500.00
Profit factor	1.85	Max # of contracts held	1
Account size required	$6,500.00	Return on account	868%

/////////////////////////// LONG TRADES - Test 1 \\\\\\\\\\\\\\\\\\\\\\\\\\\\\\

Total net profit	$30,406.25		
Gross profit	$64,406.25	Gross loss	$-34,000.00
Total # of trades	186	Percent profitable	86%
Number winning trades	161	Number losing trades	25
Largest winning trade	$1,687.50	Largest losing trade	$-1,687.50
Average winning trade	$400.04	Average losing trade	$-1,360.00
Ratio avg win/avg loss	0.29	Avg trade (win & loss)	$163.47
Max consecutive winners	16	Max consecutive losers	1
Avg # bars in winners	1	Avg # bars in losers	1

/////////////////////////// SHORT TRADES - Test 1 \\\\\\\\\\\\\\\\\\\\\\\\\\\\\\

Total net profit	$26,031.25		
Gross profit	$57,968.75	Gross loss	$-31,937.50
Total # of trades	140	Percent profitable	82%
Number winning trades	116	Number losing trades	24
Largest winning trade	$2,406.25	Largest losing trade	$-1,718.75
Average winning trade	$499.73	Average losing trade	$-1,330.73
Ratio avg win/avg loss	0.37	Avg trade (win & loss)	$185.94
Max consecutive winners	15	Max consecutive losers	3
Avg # bars in winners	1	Avg # bars in losers	3
Max closed-out drawdown	$-3,812.50	Max intra-day drawdown	$-3,812.50
Profit factor	1.81	Max # of contracts held	1
Account size required	$6,812.50	Return on account	382%

Figure 4.8   Trading on Mondays

```
Data        : S&P 500 IND-9967    01/80
Calc Dates  : 07/02/82 - 08/25/98                        Mondays

Num. Conv. P. Value  Comm  Slippage  Margin  Format  Drive:\Path\FileName
-----------------------------------------------------------------------
149    2  $   2.500  $  0  $  0   $  3,000  CT/PC   C:\GD\BACK67MS\F59.DAT

//////////////////////////// ALL TRADES  - Test 5 \\\\\\\\\\\\\\\\\\\\\\\\\\\

Total net profit         $75,712.50
Gross profit            $167,200.00   Gross loss              $-91,487.50

Total # of trades             347     Percent profitable             85%
Number winning trades         298     Number losing trades            49

Largest winning trade    $4,975.00    Largest losing trade     $-4,400.00
Average winning trade      $561.07    Average losing trade     $-1,867.09
Ratio avg win/avg loss        0.30    Avg trade (win & loss)     $218.19

Max consecutive winners        26     Max consecutive losers           3
Avg # bars in winners           1     Avg # bars in losers             3

Max closed-out drawdown  $-9,150.00   Max intra-day drawdown   $-9,750.00
Profit factor                 1.82    Max # of contracts held          1
Account size required    $12,750.00   Return on account             593%
```

Figure 4.9   Trading on Tuesdays

```
Data        : S&P 500 IND-9967    01/80
Calc Dates  : 07/02/82 - 08/25/98                        Tuesdays

Num. Conv. P. Value  Comm  Slippage  Margin  Format  Drive:\Path\FileName
-----------------------------------------------------------------------
149    2  $   2.500  $  0  $  0   $  3,000  CT/PC   C:\GD\BACK67MS\F59.DAT

//////////////////////////// ALL TRADES  - Test 1 \\\\\\\\\\\\\\\\\\\\\\\\\\\

Total net profit         $63,075.00
Gross profit            $150,725.00   Gross loss              $-87,650.00

Total # of trades             294     Percent profitable             83%
Number winning trades         246     Number losing trades            48

Largest winning trade    $8,512.50    Largest losing trade     $-3,962.50
Average winning trade      $612.70    Average losing trade     $-1,826.04
Ratio avg win/avg loss        0.33    Avg trade (win & loss)     $214.54

Max consecutive winners        24     Max consecutive losers           2
Avg # bars in winners           1     Avg # bars in losers             3

Max closed-out drawdown $-10,800.00   Max intra-day drawdown  $-10,800.00
Profit factor                 1.71    Max # of contracts held          1
Account size required    $13,800.00   Return on account             457%
```

Figure 4.10   Trading on Wednesdays

```
Data        : S&P 500 IND-9967    01/80
Calc Dates  : 07/02/82 - 08/25/98            Wednesdays

Num. Conv. P. Value  Comm  Slippage  Margin  Format  Drive:\Path\FileName
------------------------------------------------------------------------
 149   2  $  2.500  $  0   $  0   $ 3,000  CT/PC   C:\GD\BACK67MS\F59.DAT

//////////////////////////// ALL TRADES  - Test 2 \\\\\\\\\\\\\\\\\\\\\\\\\\\\\

Total net profit        $73,297.50
Gross profit           $163,372.50   Gross loss           $-90,075.00

Total # of trades            326     Percent profitable          85%
Number winning trades        278     Number losing trades         48

Largest winning trade    $4,462.50   Largest losing trade   $-3,912.50
Average winning trade      $587.67   Average losing trade   $-1,876.56
Ratio avg win/avg loss        0.31   Avg trade (win & loss)    $224.84

Max consecutive winners       28     Max consecutive losers        3
Avg # bars in winners          1     Avg # bars in losers          3

Max closed-out drawdown  $-6,762.50  Max intra-day drawdown  $-7,187.50
Profit factor                 1.81   Max # of contracts held        1
Account size required   $10,187.50   Return on account           719%
```

Figure 4.11   Trading on Thursdays

```
Data        : S&P 500 IND-9967    01/80
Calc Dates  : 07/02/82 - 08/25/98            Thursdays

Num. Conv. P. Value  Comm  Slippage  Margin  Format  Drive:\Path\FileName
------------------------------------------------------------------------
 149   2  $  2.500  $  0   $  0   $ 3,000  CT/PC   C:\GD\BACK67MS\F59.DAT

//////////////////////////// ALL TRADES  - Test 3 \\\\\\\\\\\\\\\\\\\\\\\\\\\\\

Total net profit        $56,400.00
Gross profit           $152,175.00   Gross loss           $-95,775.00

Total # of trades            307     Percent profitable          84%
Number winning trades        260     Number losing trades         47

Largest winning trade    $6,687.50   Largest losing trade   $-5,575.00
Average winning trade      $585.29   Average losing trade   $-2,037.77
Ratio avg win/avg loss        0.28   Avg trade (win & loss)    $183.71

Max consecutive winners       30     Max consecutive losers        2
Avg # bars in winners          2     Avg # bars in losers          3

Max closed-out drawdown  $-9,700.00  Max intra-day drawdown $-12,537.50
Profit factor                 1.58   Max # of contracts held        1
Account size required   $15,537.50   Return on account           362%
```

Figure 4.12   Trading on Fridays

```
Data        : S&P 500 IND-9967    01/80
Calc Dates  : 07/02/82 - 08/25/98                          Fridays

Num. Conv. P. Value  Comm  Slippage  Margin  Format  Drive:\Path\FileName
------------------------------------------------------------------------
 149   2  $  2.500   $  0   $  0    $ 3,000  CT/PC   C:\GD\BACK67MS\F59.DAT

///////////////////////////// ALL TRADES  - Test 4 \\\\\\\\\\\\\\\\\\\\\\\\\\\\

Total net profit          $60,162.50
Gross profit             $148,387.50    Gross loss              $-88,225.00

Total # of trades               297    Percent profitable              86%
Number winning trades           256    Number losing trades             41

Largest winning trade      $4,387.50    Largest losing trade     $-8,800.00
Average winning trade        $579.64    Average losing trade     $-2,151.83
Ratio avg win/avg loss         0.26    Avg trade (win & loss)      $202.57

Max consecutive winners          21    Max consecutive losers            2
Avg # bars in winners             1    Avg # bars in losers              3

Max closed-out drawdown  $-13,125.00    Max intra-day drawdown  $-13,125.00
Profit factor                  1.68    Max # of contracts held           1
Account size required     $16,125.00    Return on account              373%
```

Figure 4.13   Short trades test: Monday

```
///////////////////////////// SHORT TRADES  - Test 5 \\\\\\\\\\\\\\\\\\\\\\\\\\\\
Total net profit          $-4,812.50          Monday
Gross profit             $135,525.00    Gross loss             -140,337.50

Total # of trades               277    Percent profitable              73%
Number winning trades           203    Number losing trades             74

Largest winning trade     $16,712.50    Largest losing trade     $-5,875.00
Average winning trade        $667.61    Average losing trade     $-1,896.45
Ratio avg win/avg loss         0.35    Avg trade (win & loss)      $-17.37

Max consecutive winners          27    Max consecutive losers            5
Avg # bars in winners             2    Avg # bars in losers              4

Max closed-out drawdown  $-26,225.00    Max intra-day drawdown  $-26,900.00
Profit factor                  0.96    Max # of contracts held           1
Account size required     $29,900.00    Return on account              -16%
```

Figure 4.14   Short trades test: Tuesday

```
/////////////////////////////// SHORT TRADES  - Test 1 \\\\\\\\\\\\\\\\\\\\\\\\\\\\\
Total net profit        $-21,400.00          Tuesday
Gross profit            $142,825.00   Gross loss              -164,225.00

Total # of trades             329     Percent profitable           75%
Number winning trades         248     Number losing trades           81

Largest winning trade     $9,987.50   Largest losing trade    $-14,125.00
Average winning trade       $575.91   Average losing trade     $-2,027.47
Ratio avg win/avg loss         0.28   Avg trade (win & loss)     $-65.05

Max consecutive winners        15     Max consecutive losers          4
Avg # bars in winners           2     Avg # bars in losers            3

Max closed-out drawdown $-37,275.00   Max intra-day drawdown  $-37,975.00
Profit factor                  0.86   Max # of contracts held         1
Account size required   $40,975.00    Return on account            -52%
```

Figure 4.15   Short trades test: Wednesday

```
/////////////////////////////// SHORT TRADES  - Test 2 \\\\\\\\\\\\\\\\\\\\\\\\\\\\\
Total net profit        $-15,987.50          Wednesday
Gross profit            $141,512.50   Gross loss              -157,500.00

Total # of trades             312     Percent profitable           74%
Number winning trades         232     Number losing trades           80

Largest winning trade     $4,837.50   Largest losing trade     $-4,975.00
Average winning trade       $609.97   Average losing trade     $-1,968.75
Ratio avg win/avg loss         0.30   Avg trade (win & loss)     $-51.24

Max consecutive winners        22     Max consecutive losers          3
Avg # bars in winners           2     Avg # bars in losers            3

Max closed-out drawdown $-24,737.50   Max intra-day drawdown  $-25,475.00
Profit factor                  0.89   Max # of contracts held         1
Account size required   $28,475.00    Return on account            -56%
```

Figure 4.16   Short trades test: Thursday

```
/////////////////////////////// SHORT TRADES  - Test 3 \\\\\\\\\\\\\\\\\\\\\\\\\\\\\
Total net profit         $36,250.00          Thursday
Gross profit            $183,775.00   Gross loss              -147,525.00

Total # of trades             318     Percent profitable           75%
Number winning trades         241     Number losing trades           77

Largest winning trade     $8,737.50   Largest losing trade     $-4,212.50
Average winning trade       $762.55   Average losing trade     $-1,915.91
Ratio avg win/avg loss         0.39   Avg trade (win & loss)     $113.99

Max consecutive winners        19     Max consecutive losers          5
Avg # bars in winners           1     Avg # bars in losers            3

Max closed-out drawdown $-12,950.00   Max intra-day drawdown  $-13,187.50
Profit factor                  1.24   Max # of contracts held         1
Account size required   $16,187.50    Return on account            223%
```

Figure 4.17   Short trades test: Friday

```
///////////////////////////// SHORT TRADES  - Test 4 \\\\\\\\\\\\\\\\\\\\\\\\\\\\\
Total net profit         $26,350.00         Friday
Gross profit             $182,400.00    Gross loss              -156,050.00

Total # of trades            347        Percent profitable          76%
Number winning trades        267        Number losing trades         80

Largest winning trade    $9,262.50      Largest losing trade    $-4,250.00
Average winning trade    $683.15        Average losing trade    $-1,950.62
Ratio avg win/avg loss   0.35           Avg trade (win & loss)      $75.94

Max consecutive winners      42         Max consecutive losers        4
Avg # bars in winners         1         Avg # bars in losers          2

Max closed-out drawdown  $-32,812.50    Max intra-day drawdown  $-32,812.50
Profit factor            1.16           Max # of contracts held       1
Account size required    $35,812.50     Return on account            73%
```

Figure 4.18   Trading on more influential days

```
Data       : S&P 500 IND-9967    01/80
Calc Dates : 07/02/82 - 08/25/98

Num. Conv. P. Value  Comm  Slippage  Margin  Format  Drive:\Path\FileName
------------------------------------------------------------------------
149   2  $  2.500  $  0   $  0    $  3,000  CT/PC   C:\GD\BACK67MS\F59.DAT

///////////////////////////// ALL TRADES  - Test 1 \\\\\\\\\\\\\\\\\\\\\\\\\\\\\
Total net profit         $227,822.50
Gross profit             $642,447.50    Gross loss              -414,625.00

Total # of trades          1,333        Percent profitable          74%
Number winning trades        993        Number losing trades        340

Largest winning trade    $8,737.50      Largest losing trade    $-4,400.00
Average winning trade    $646.98        Average losing trade    $-1,219.49
Ratio avg win/avg loss   0.53           Avg trade (win & loss)     $170.91

Max consecutive winners      24         Max consecutive losers        4
Avg # bars in winners         1         Avg # bars in losers          1

Max closed-out drawdown  $-13,737.50    Max intra-day drawdown  $-13,737.50
Profit factor            1.54           Max # of contracts held       1
Account size required    $16,737.50     Return on account         1,361%
```

Figure 4.19   Research pays off

```
Data            : S&P 500 IND-9967    01/80
Calc Dates      : 07/02/82 - 08/25/98

Num. Conv. P. Value  Comm  Slippage  Margin  Format  Drive:\Path\FileName
-------------------------------------------------------------------------
 149   2   $  2.500  $  0   $  0    $ 3,000   CT/PC  C:\GD\BACK67MS\F59.DAT

/////////////////////////////// ALL TRADES  - Test 68 \\\\\\\\\\\\\\\\\\\\\\\\\\\\
Total net profit        $213,560.00
Gross profit            $473,110.00   Gross loss                -259,550.00

Total # of trades              850    Percent profitable               83%
Number winning trades          709    Number losing trades             141

Largest winning trade   $10,250.00    Largest losing trade      $-6,850.00
Average winning trade      $667.29    Average losing trade      $-1,840.78
Ratio avg win/avg loss        0.36    Avg trade (win & loss)       $251.25

Max consecutive winners         40    Max consecutive losers             3
Avg # bars in winners            1    Avg # bars in losers               2

Max closed-out drawdown  $-9,712.50   Max intra-day drawdown   $-10,087.50
Profit factor                  1.82   Max # of contracts held            1
Account size required   $13,087.50    Return on account             1,631%
```

83 percent, the average profit per trade is escalated to $251, and our number of trades is reduced by 46 percent!

Separating Buyers from Sellers to Find Volatility Using Market Swings

Another way to measure potential volatility expansions comes from looking at price swings over the past several days. Mike Chalek deserves credit for this concept with a system he designed and labeled, "Talon." The basic idea is to look at the various swings price has taken from one point to the next over the past few years. There are many such points to study.

The ones I have chosen for this next glimpse into market activity, measure the amount of price movement from the high 3 days ago to today's low. That is Step 1. Step 2 is to take the swing distance from the high 1 day ago minus the low 3 days ago. Finally, we will use the largest of these values as our basic volatility measurement to begin the process of designing a filter or price cushion to add to tomorrow's opening for buying or subtract for selling.

Figure 4.20 Using market swings

```
Data          : S&P 500 IND-9967    01/80
Calc Dates    : 07/02/82 - 08/25/98

Num. Conv. P. Value  Comm  Slippage  Margin  Format  Drive:\Path\FileName
---------------------------------------------------------------------------
  149    2  $  2.500  $  0  $  0   $  3,000  CT/PC  C:\GD\BACK67MS\F59.DAT

//////////////////////////// ALL TRADES  - Test 4 \\\\\\\\\\\\\\\\\\\\\\\\\\\\

Total net profit        $122,837.50
Gross profit            $264,937.50   Gross loss              -142,100.00

Total # of trades              538    Percent profitable              84%
Number winning trades          454    Number losing trades            84

Largest winning trade    $10,675.00   Largest losing trade     $-8,150.00
Average winning trade       $583.56   Average losing trade     $-1,691.67
Ratio avg win/avg loss         0.34   Avg trade (win & loss)     $228.32

Max consecutive winners         83    Max consecutive losers            5
Avg # bars in winners            1    Avg # bars in losers              2

Max closed-out drawdown  $-13,025.00  Max intra-day drawdown   $-13,112.50
Profit factor                  1.86   Max # of contracts held           1
Account size required    $16,112.50   Return on account              762%
```

The system does okay; it makes money as the results on the S&P 500 from 1982 to 1998 demonstrate (see Figure 4.20). The rules are to buy at 80 percent of the swing value above the opening and sell at 120 percent of the swing value below the opening. Use a dollar stop of $1,750 and my bailout exit. This makes $122,837 from 1982 to 1998 with an average profit per trade of $228.

Results

As always though, the question becomes, can we do better? Our last attempt at doing better was to use TDW as our filter to substantially improve performance. We will now go beyond this and bring in a fundamental consideration—the impact of bond prices on stock prices.

We will now try this concept as a filter (Figure 4.21). The rule is quite simple, we will only take buy signals if the closing price of bonds is greater today than 5 days ago, and only take sells if bonds are lower than 35 days ago. Our reasoning is well founded in the somewhat common knowledge that higher bond prices are bullish for stocks, lower bond prices bearish.

Figure 4.21   The impact of bond prices on stock prices

```
Data             : S&P 500 IND-9967   01/80
Calc Dates       : 07/02/82 - 08/25/98

Num. Conv. P. Value  Comm  Slippage  Margin  Format  Drive:\Path\FileName
------------------------------------------------------------------------
 149   2  $  2.500  $  0   $  0   $  3,000  CT/PC  C:\GD\BACK67MS\F59.DAT

////////////////////////// ALL TRADES  - Test 7 \\\\\\\\\\\\\\\\\\\\\\\\\\\
```

Total net profit	$82,987.50		
Gross profit	$148,350.00	Gross loss	$-65,362.50
Total # of trades	295	Percent profitable	87%
Number winning trades	258	Number losing trades	37
Largest winning trade	$10,675.00	Largest losing trade	$-2,075.00
Average winning trade	$575.00	Average losing trade	$-1,766.55
Ratio avg win/avg loss	0.32	Avg trade (win & loss)	$281.31
Max consecutive winners	59	Max consecutive losers	3
Avg # bars in winners	1	Avg # bars in losers	3
Max closed-out drawdown	$-5,250.00	Max intra-day drawdown	$-5,250.00
Profit factor	2.26	Max # of contracts held	1
Account size required	$8,250.00	Return on account	1,005%

What a difference this makes! An average profit per trade goes from $228 to $281 while our drawdown plummets from $13,025 to only $5,250. Best of all though is that in the original "nonfiltered" trades we had a largest losing trade of $8,150, whereas with the bond filter the largest loss was only $2,075!

One Step Further

Your education is nearing completion if you are wondering what happens in this model if we only take signals on the best TDWs while the trend of the Bond market is giving us bullish or bearish confirmation?

Again, the results speak for themselves: By combining all these ingredients, we increase our chances or odds for day trading success. Notice the number of trades is substantially reduced; this means our exposure is less, but our average profit per trade increases. Our profits decline to "only" $76,400 but the average profit per trade jumps to $444, drawdown stays about the same at $5,912 but the percentage of winning trades goes to 90 percent.

What we have done here is filter out trades that are not backed by all three of our conditions. Filtered trading for short-term swings will put you a light year—or two—ahead of all the rest of the day traders. There is an extra advantage here; by using filters you are placing demands on the market that mean you will not trade too much, demands that naturally force you to trade less, not more. Those of us who pick and choose our spots to speculate are more inclined to come out winners as we have tipped the scales in our favor, which is what intelligent speculation is all about.

chapter 5

the theory of
day trading

Now that you have a basic strategy of how to best take advantage of swings in the market, it is time to examine the theory of what we are doing; I can then take you back to practical application.

Our basic concept or working theory is that something causes explosive market moves. These explosions put the market into a trend phase, and these trends, for our purpose, last from 1 to 5 days in most markets. Our object is to get aboard as close to the start of this explosion as possible.

Which gives rise to the questions, "What causes these explosions in market activity, when are they most apt to occur, and is there anything here we can use to pin down the time and place of these moves?"

Succinctly stated, those are the problems I have dealt with most of my life. Long ago, I recognized that if I could not identify a problem there was no way on earth I could find its solution. You now know the problems so let's look for some solutions. Let me hastily add that I do not have all the answers to this gigantic puzzle. There is nothing like losing to bring you to your senses, to teach you that you are not so damned smart, that you need more education. I still have losses, plenty of them, so I too, still need more education—and always will.

In the previous section, we discussed how to trade the news. Trading price action can be used in conjunction with the news to define entry points or to see if the news is already in the price. Price action can also be used all by itself to trade the models. The nice thing about price action, as reflected on charts, is that there are plenty of things to look at and analyze, the most common being (1) price patterns, (2) indicators based on price action, and (3) the trend or momentum of price. Not so common, and the fourth one of my big tools, is the relationship one market may have on another. Remember the S&P 500 system and how much better it was when we required that bonds be in an uptrend? That is an example of market relationships that I discuss in detail a little later on.

Our final and fifth set of data to key off of comes from following the crowd most often found to be wrong. On a short-term basis, the great unwashed public trader is a net loser. Always has been, always will be. The figures I have heard bandied about over the years are that 80 percent of the public lose all their money, be they stock or commodity traders. Thus coppering their wagers should lead us to those short-term explosions and profits. There are various ways to measure the public; these are called *sentiment indicators*. The two best ones I know of are surveys of the public done by Jake Bernstein and Market Vane.

For day traders, I prefer Jake's because he actually calls 50 traders after the close each day to find out if they are bullish or bearish on any given market. Since these are short-term traders, and by definition usually wrong, we can use them as a guide of when not to be a buyer or seller. I will not use them exclusively as an indicator to buy or sell, but as a tool that should not be in agreement with my own hand-selected trade. If the public is excessive in their selling, I don't want to be a seller along with them. I may not always fade the public, but I sure don't want them on my side of the table.

Market Vane takes sentiment readings from newsletter writers as opposed to short-term traders; thus their index appears to be better suited for a longer term view of things.

Well, there you have it, the five major elements I have found that can help with ferreting out short-term explosions. We will overlay these "tools" or events on market structure to enable us to hop aboard up and down moves. Since all these tools can be quantified, the logical procedure is to convert these observations and tools into mathematical models. The next leap of logic traders make is that since math is always perfect (two plus two always equals four), there must be a perfect solution to trading and mathematics can provide the answer.

Nothing could be more distant from the truth. There is not a 100 percent correct mechanical approach to trading. There are tools and techniques that, based on observation, usually work, but the reason we lose money is that we either reached an incorrect conclusion or did not have enough data to make a correct one. So math is not the answer, mechanics is not the answer. The truth of the market comes from ample observations, a dose of logic, and correct conclusions from the data at hand.

I am telling you this right up front so you do not get lulled into the idea that speculation is a game of blindly following the leader, a system, or absolute approach. If any one thing is certain about the markets it is that things change. In the early 1960s, an increase in money supply figures was considered very bullish and always put stock prices higher. For whatever reason, in the late 1970s and early 1980s, an increase in money supply figures, as released from that largest of all privately held corporations the Federal Reserve, put stock prices down. In the 1990 time period, money supply is barely looked at or felt in the marketplace. What was once sacred became apparently meaningless.

One of the markets I trade the most heavily in, Bonds, traded totally differently after 1988 than prior to that date. Why? Prior to October of that year there was only one trading session, then we went into night sessions and eventually almost a 24-hour market. That changed trading patterns. What is more confusing to researchers is that "in the old days" the Fed released reports on Thursday that had a huge impact on Friday's Bond prices. This effect was so great, a popular novel used it as the central theme of a Wall Street swindle. As I write this, there are no Thursday reports, hence Fridays look and trade differently now.

If you are to do me any favor as a reader of my work, you will not only learn my basic tools but also learn to stay awake and current to what is happening. Great traders, which I hope you become, are smart enough to note and respond to changes. They do not lock themselves into a "black box" unchangeable trading approach.

One of the truly great traders from 1960 to 1983 was a former professional baseball player, Frankie Joe. Frankie had a great wit and a deep understanding of his approach to trading. He was quite a guy, sharp as a tack and a delight to talk with. After we had developed a three-year friendship, he revealed to me his technique, it was to sell rallies and buy back on dips in the stock market. That is all there was to it; no more, no less. This was a great technique during that time period, it amassed a fortune for Frankie.

Then along came the most predictable, yet unpredictable, bull market of all time triggered by Ronald Reagan's tax and budgetary cuts. It was quite predictable that the bull market would come about. What no one realized was that there would be no pullbacks along the way as we had seen for the previous 18 years. Not even one of the greatest traders of all time, Frankie Joe. He kept selling rallies and was never able to cover on dips; there just weren't any. Eventually, he became so frustrated with losses and the lack of success (like all great traders, he was also compulsive about winning), that he apparently committed suicide.

What works, works in this business, but often not for long, which is why I so admire ballerinas: They stay on their toes.

What Is Wrong about the Information Age

Fundamental principles do not change—that is why they are called fundamentals. "Do unto others as you would have others do unto you," was good advice 2,000 years ago and will be good advice 2,000 years from now. The principles I'm laying out in this book are enduring; I have lived with them for close to 40 years and have literally made millions of dollars trading.

Yet, were I to fall into a coma today and wake up 10 years from now I might not use the exact same rules with these fundamental principles. Whereas fundamentals are permanent, the application and specifics do change and will vary.

Technology has become king, speeding up every facet of life. We can now learn about anything faster, communicate faster, and find out about price changes faster. Indeed, we can buy and sell faster; get rich quicker; go broke faster; and lie, cheat, and steal at unbelievable speeds. We can even get sick or healed faster than ever before in the history of the world!

Traders have never had so much information and so much ability to process this information. Thanks to the products detailed in this book—most notably from Omega research—average Joes like you and me can now test market ideas.

But guess what? We still have the same numbers of winners and losers. Guys and gals with state-of-the-art computers still get blown out on a regular basis. The difference between winners and losers largely occurs because winners are willing to work, to notice changes, and to react. Losers want it all without effort; they fall for the pitch of a perfect system and an unchanging guru or indicator they are willing to follow blindly. Losers don't listen to others or to the market; they are unyielding in their minds and trades.

On top of that, they consistently fail to abide by the fundamental of successful business, which is to never plunge, to manage your money as well as your business by getting rid of bad deals and keeping the good ones. Me? I will stick to the fundamentals, as taught, with a healthy willingness to adapt to change. When I stay flexible, I do not get bent out of shape.

E. H. Harriman's Rule of Making Millions

The Harriman family fortune, which endures to this day, was created in the early 1900s by "Old Man Harriman," who had started his career as a floor runner and went on to become a major banking and brokerage power. He made a $15 million profit in 1905 from one play in Union Pacific. This speculator king focused on just railroad stocks, the hot issue of his era.

In 1912, an interviewer asked Harriman about his stock market skills and secrets. The trader replied, "If you want to know the secret of making money in the stock market, it is this: Kill your losses. Never let a stock run against you more than three-quarters of a point, but if it goes your way, let it run. Move your stops up behind it so that it will have room to fluctuate and move higher."

Harriman learned his cardinal rule from studying trading accounts of customers at a brokerage firm. What he discovered was that of the thousands upon thousands of trades in the public accounts, 5- and 10-point losses outnumbered 5- and 10-point gains. He said, "by fifty to one!" It has always amazed me that businesspeople who have tight control and accounting practices in their stores and offices lose all control when it comes to trading. I cannot think of a higher authority than E. H. Harriman, nor a more enduring rule of speculation than what this man gave us in 1912.

Like I said, fundamentals don't change.

chapter 6

patterns to profit

Chartists have believed that certain patterns or formations on their charts can predict market behavior. For the most part, this crowd has looked at long-term patterns of market activity. Serious students of such phenomena should start with the Edwards and Magee classic, *Technical Analysis of Stock Trends*.

In the 1930s, Richard Wyckoff, Owen Taylor, Gartley and George Seaman (my favorite), spent a great deal of time on these long-term patterns in an attempt to build a systematic approach to trading. In the 1950s, Richard Dunnigan took a big step forward by focusing on price patterns of 10 to 15 days while the older crowd was still looking at 30- to 60-day price patterns.

As mentioned, these same price patterns can be found in any chartable activity. Flip a coin, chart it, and you will see the same formations found on a Pork Belly or Corn chart! This has turned some analysts away from price structure analysis and for good reason; generally speaking, these patterns do not forecast or tell us much about the future. This may be because there is no predictable ability in chart formations, or the time period studied is not correct. W. L. Linden, writing in *Forbes* magazine, found that economic forecasts made by leading economists have consistently been incorrect at virtually every major turning point since the 1970s. A chilling thought here is that the study included forecasts done by Townsend-Greenspan—the latter name is that of the man who became head of the Federal Reserve System (the world's most powerful private corporation), Alan Greenspan.

The only ray of hope to be found in the article is the statement that these forecasts were correct in only a short time frame. This makes sense; it is far easier to forecast the next 5 minutes of your life than the next 5 years. As time progresses, more variables, more change, come into play. Hence forecasts stumble in the unknown dark, black holes of the future altering what was once known or thought to be the path of righteousness.

I guess this may explain why I have actually made money (for many years I might add), trading off of patterns. The patterns I have used are for calling very short-term market fluctuations of from 1 to 5 days. There may be some grand scheme of things, some master pattern of all major market highs and lows. If so, it has never been revealed to me, but certainly there are many short-term market patterns that give you a big—in some cases, I would go so far as saying huge—advantage in the game.

The Common Element

First, I need to prove that patterns can and do work or at least bring an advantage to the table, a cow for us to milk. Then I can tell you why I think these patterns do work, what the method to the madness is, what my working premise to these patterns to profits is all about.

Let's start with a basic pattern using the S&P 500, a broadly traded market. What we know is that 50 percent of the time this market should close up for the day, 50 percent of the time down for the day. What will happen tomorrow on any given day is supposed to be a coin flip, if we don't consider TDW.

Patterns can change all that rather dramatically.

We begin by establishing a basic parameter. What happens if we buy the S&P 500 every day and exit on the next close with a $3,250 stop? From July 1982 through February 1998, there were 2,064 trades with 52 percent accuracy and an average profit per trade of $134.

Now we add our first pattern, what if we only buy tomorrow if today closed down? In this case, there were 1,334 trades with the same 52 percent accuracy, but the average profit per trade escalated to $212. Finally, if our pattern consists of three consecutive down closes, the accuracy jumps to 58 percent to 248 trades and the average profit per trade skyrockets to $353! Could it be there is something to this pattern stuff?

Let's mock up a simple pattern to see what happens tomorrow if the following conditions exist: First, we want today's price to be greater than the close 30 days ago so we are in some sort of uptrend. Next, we would like to have seen a slight pullback against the uptrend so we will want today's close lower than the close 9 days ago. If that condition exists, we will buy on the open tomorrow and exit on the next day's close. If the market is really random, 52 percent of such trades should make money (not 50% because during the time period of the study there had been an overall trend bias to rally best evidenced by the fact that the initial study showed higher closes 52% of the time).

The facts of the matter are far different. This meek little pattern produced 354 trades with 57 percent accuracy and an average profit of $421 a trade. Accuracy jumps from 52 percent to 57 percent and the average profit per trade increases almost fourfold! Hold on to your hat, it gets better. But first, I'd like to reiterate that this pattern could cetainly work on intraday charts. The key is testing, testing, testing.

If we combine a pattern with our trade-day-of-the-week concept and take these pattern trades on just Monday, the accuracy goes to 59 percent and average profit to $672. I rest my case; patterns and days of the week can be a helpful trading tool or advantage for the short-term trader as of course, trading hours of the day can be as well:

> The best patterns I have found have a common element tying them together: Patterns that represent extreme market emotions reliably set up trades for price swings in the opposite direction.

In other words, what the public "sees" on their charts as being negative is most often apt to be positive for short-term market moves and vice versa. A case in point is an outside day with a down close. The day's high is greater than the previous day's high and the low is lower than the previous day's low and the close is below the previous day's low. This looks bad, like the sky is indeed falling. In fact, the books I have read say this is an excellent sell signal, that such a wild swing is a sign of a market reversal in favor of the direction of the close, in this case down.

Whoever writes these books does not spend much time looking at price charts! As Figure 6.1 of the Dollar Index shows, this can be a very bullish pattern or market configuration.

Figure 6.1   U.S. dollar (daily bars). Graphed by the "Navigator" (Genesis Financial Data Services)

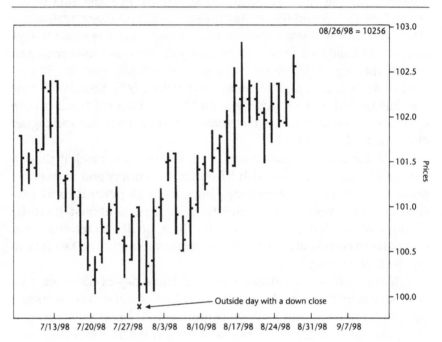

Reality is far different than conjecture as a quick computer test shows and reveals the power of one of my favorite short-term patterns. It does not take much to prove the validity of patterns or to check to see what is really going on. Given this outside day pattern I have noticed, there is a final filter, or event, that can happen to further influence the pattern tomorrow. This event is the direction of tomorrow's opening, as shown in Figure 6.2. If, in the S&P 500 index, tomorrow opens lower than the outside day's down close and we buy on the next day's opening, we find 109 occurrences with 85 percent accuracy making $52,062 and $477 a trade.

If we buy on any day but Thursday, a day we know tends to see selling pressures spilling over into Friday, we make a little less, $50,037 but bump our average profit per trade up to $555 and increase accuracy to 86 percent with drawdown going from $8,000 to $6,000. These results use a $2,000 stop to exit or the first profitable opening exit rule (see Figure 6.3).

Figure 6.2 A bullish pattern

```
Data            : S&P 500 IND-9967    01/80
Calc Dates      : 07/02/82 - 08/27/98

Num. Conv. P. Value  Comm  Slippage  Margin  Format  Drive:\Path\FileName
-----------------------------------------------------------------------------
149   2   $   2.500  $  0   $   0   $  3,000  CT/PC   C:\GD\BACK67MS\F59.DAT

//////////////////////////// ALL TRADES  - Test 1 \\\\\\\\\\\\\\\\\\\\\\\\\\\

Total net profit          $52,062.50
Gross profit              $84,062.50   Gross loss                $-32,000.00

Total # of trades               109   Percent profitable                85%
Number winning trades            93   Number losing trades               16

Largest winning trade     $4,887.50   Largest losing trade       $-2,000.00
Average winning trade        $903.90   Average losing trade       $-2,000.00
Ratio avg win/avg loss          0.45   Avg trade (win & loss)        $477.64

Max consecutive winners          44   Max consecutive losers              4
Avg # bars in winners             2   Avg # bars in losers                1

Max closed-out drawdown   $-8,000.00   Max intra-day drawdown     $-8,000.00
Profit factor                  2.62   Max # of contracts held             1
Account size required     $11,000.00   Return on account                473%
```

We can use this same pattern for setting up trading opportunities in the Bond market as well. This pattern is so powerful that it can be used in all markets as a stand-alone trading formation, but stacked-deck Larry still prefers to have additional confirmation to make certain I use only the best of the best trades. Figure 6.4 shows

Figure 6.3 Using the first profitable opening exit rule

```
Data            : S&P 500 IND-9967    01/80
Calc Dates      : 07/02/82 - 08/27/98

Num. Conv. P. Value  Comm  Slippage  Margin  Format  Drive:\Path\FileName
-----------------------------------------------------------------------------
149   2   $   2.500  $  0   $   0   $  3,000  CT/PC   C:\GD\BACK67MS\F59.DAT

//////////////////////////// ALL TRADES  - Test 1 \\\\\\\\\\\\\\\\\\\\\\\\\\\

Total net profit          $50,037.50
Gross profit              $74,187.50   Gross loss                $-24,150.00

Total # of trades                90   Percent profitable                86%
Number winning trades            78   Number losing trades               12

Largest winning trade     $4,887.50   Largest losing trade       $-2,150.00
Average winning trade        $951.12   Average losing trade       $-2,012.50
Ratio avg win/avg loss          0.47   Avg trade (win & loss)        $555.97

Max consecutive winners          39   Max consecutive losers              3
Avg # bars in winners             2   Avg # bars in losers                1

Max closed-out drawdown   $-6,000.00   Max intra-day drawdown     $-6,000.00
Profit factor                  3.07   Max # of contracts held             1
Account size required      $9,000.00   Return on account                555%
```

Figure 6.4 All outside day down closes

```
Data          : DAY T-BONDS          67/99
Calc Dates    : 06/10/90 - 08/27/98

Num. Conv. P. Value  Comm  Slippage  Margin  Format  Drive:\Path\FileName
-----------------------------------------------------------------------------
 144  -3  $  31.250  $ 55  $    0    $ 3,000  CSI    C:\GD\BACK67\F061.DTA

//////////////////////////////// ALL TRADES  - Test 1 \\\\\\\\\\\\\\\\\\\\\\\\\\\\\\\\
Total net profit          $12,115.00
Gross profit              $27,665.00   Gross loss               $-15,550.00

Total # of trades                 57   Percent profitable               82%
Number winning trades             47   Number losing trades             10

Largest winning trade     $2,101.25   Largest losing trade      $-1,555.00
Average winning trade        $588.62   Average losing trade      $-1,555.00
Ratio avg win/avg loss         0.37   Avg trade (win & loss)       $212.54

Max consecutive winners           11   Max consecutive losers            3
Avg # bars in winners              2   Avg # bars in losers              1

Max closed-out drawdown   $-5,416.25   Max intra-day drawdown    $-5,510.00
Profit factor                   1.77   Max # of contracts held           1
Account size required      $8,510.00   Return on account               142%
```

the results of taking all outside day down closes followed by a lower opening the next day in Bonds. To get out of the trade, we will take a $1,500 loss or exit on the first profitable opening. Few traders realize that such a mechanical approach to trading can be so good, we score an 82 percent accuracy and $212 average profit per trade on the 57 occurrences since 1990.

Can we make this a better performing pattern? You bet. Got any ideas how? You should by now, in fact, you are probably wondering whether the pattern is better on some days of the week than others. It is. If we take the trade on any day but Thursday, just as in the previous S&P results, we skyrocket the accuracy to 90 percent and make $17,245 on 41 trades for an average profit per trade of $420 (see Figure 6.5). Folks, it doesn't get much better than this.

The problem is these outside day patterns do not occur as often as we would like! The next time you see an outside day with a down close lower than the previous day, don't get scared, get ready to buy!

Time for another bullish looking pattern in the S&P 500. We will now look for any day that closes above the previous day's high and is preceded by two consecutive up closes, making it the third up day in a row (see Figure 6.6). Such seemingly strong showings of strength have been known to lure the public into buying.

Figure 6.5   Trade on any day but Thursday

```
Data          : DAY T-BONDS        67/99
Calc Dates    : 06/10/90 - 08/27/98

Num. Conv. P. Value  Comm  Slippage  Margin  Format  Drive:\Path\FileName
-------------------------------------------------------------------------
 144   -3  $  31.250  $ 55  $   0    $ 3,000  CSI    C:\GD\BACK67\F061.DTA

/////////////////////////////// ALL TRADES  - Test 1 \\\\\\\\\\\\\\\\\\\\\\\\\\\\\\

Total net profit          $17,245.00
Gross profit              $23,465.00   Gross loss                $-6,220.00

Total # of trades                 41   Percent profitable              90%
Number winning trades             37   Number losing trades             4

Largest winning trade      $2,101.25   Largest losing trade      $-1,555.00
Average winning trade        $634.19   Average losing trade      $-1,555.00
Ratio avg win/avg loss          0.40   Avg trade (win & loss)       $420.61

Max consecutive winners           11   Max consecutive losers            1
Avg # bars in winners              2   Avg # bars in losers              1

Max closed-out drawdown   $-1,555.00   Max intra-day drawdown    $-1,555.00
Profit factor                   3.77   Max # of contracts held           1
Account size required      $4,555.00   Return on account              378%
```

Figure 6.6   A close that is above the day's high

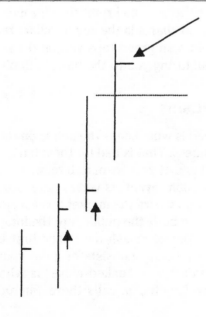

For example, checking this pattern from 1986 to 1998 in the S&P 500, there were 25 occurrences of this pattern on Tuesday setting up sells for Wednesday. Of these, 19 were winners, netting $21,487. In the Bond market, the same pattern set up 28 trades on Thursday, to sell on Friday, making $13,303 which challenges the random walk professors with a thought-provoking 89 percent accuracy. The Bond test was on data from 1989 to August 1998! A $1,500 stop was used in Bonds, $2,000 in the S&P 500.

For both markets, we used the simple bailout exit I will teach later. There are several major short-term patterns like this that I take advantage of in my trading. The search is on each day to see what the current pattern foretells. I have some stock patterns that I have used for years, but am always on the lookout for new ones.

The Questions to Ask

Patterns work. I know. I have cataloged hundreds of them over the years and suggest you do the same starting with the ones I am providing here. It is best to think about why these patterns work. What do they represent? Can I find the pattern at work in all markets? Does the trading day of the week matter? Those are my stock questions, but the underlying germ of truth I am looking for is some visual pattern that emotionally sucks the public into buying or selling at just the wrong time . . . for them . . . and right time for me. Understanding emotions as reflected on charts is the key to "chart reading."

The next time old man greed taps you on the shoulder or you hear an emotional call luring you to the bait . . . don't bite!

My Smash Day Patterns

The siren song of greed is what keeps the public on the losing side of the ledger in this business. That is bad for them but good for us if we can figure out what it is that gets them to bite, what sucks them into wrong decisions. One such "event" is what I have labeled smash day reversals. These are days where the market has a major break, up or down; this violent action pulls the public into the foray.

There are two types of smash days. The first is pretty obvious. A "smash day buy setup" consists of a day that closes lower than the previous day's low, a "naked close" is what Joe Stowell, who's got a great eye for charts, calls these. Such days may take out the previous 3 to 8 days' lows as well. To the chartist, the public, or professional technical analyst, this looks like a breakout to the downside, thus the extreme selling brings them to the table.

Sometimes they are right, but usually dead wrong if the market immediately reverses itself.

A smash day sell setup is just the opposite (see Figure 6.7). Here what you will be looking for is a day that closes above the prior day's high and most likely "breaks" out to the upside to close above a trading range. This is the twitching worm that causes the public to leap before they look. The illustration shows how this usually looks. What you have here are the buy and sell setups.

As mentioned, sometimes this is a valid break. However, if *the very next day* price moves opposite the smash day and trades above the high of a down close smash day, you have a great buy signal. By the same token, a smash day up, one of those strong closes above the prior day's high, alerts us to sell signal if *the very next day* price trades to the smash day's low.

The phenomenon is that there is an immediate reversal the very next day, which means the public (sellers on the down close, buyers on the up close) are now in a world of hurt; their envisioned breakout has failed! They swallowed the hook, again, and now price

Figure 6.7 A smash day sell setup

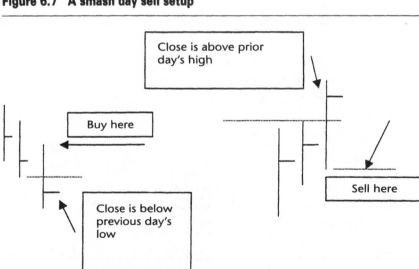

responds with a reversal giving us an excellent entry. That is the pattern and the rationale, the reason it should work. I am a firm believer that when what "should happen in the market doesn't" we have powerful evidence to take a trade in alignment with the new information.

I have selected a few examples of this pattern at work (Figures 6.8 and 6.9). Once we review the other type of smash day reversal, I will explain how I use this pattern.

My second smash day reversal (Figure 6.10) is a bit more difficult to identify but works on the same principle of the market not following through on one day's action and reversing the very next day. The pattern you will be looking for, to establish a buy setup, will be a day that has an up close, *not a naked down close*. But, and this is the key or secret to the pattern, the day's close will be in the lower 25 percent of the up day's range and will also be closing below the opening of the day in the very best patterns. I call this a "hidden smash day" because of the up close.

What has happened on these days is that price has either opened much higher and then closed up for the day but way off the highs, or opened a little higher, rallied way up and then failed to hold the day's gains. Sure, it closed up a little for the day but way

---

Figure 6.8 Smash day pattern at work

```
Data          : S&P 500 IND-9967    01/80
Calc Dates    : 07/02/82 - 08/27/98

Num. Conv. P. Value  Comm  Slippage  Margin  Format  Drive:\Path\FileName
-------------------------------------------------------------------------
149    2  $   2.500  $  0  $   0    $ 3,000  CT/PC   C:\GD\BACK67MS\F59.DAT

///////////////////////////// ALL TRADES - Test 2 \\\\\\\\\\\\\\\\\\\\\\\\\\\\\\
Total net profit        $21,487.50
Gross profit            $33,487.50    Gross loss             $-12,000.00

Total # of trades             25     Percent profitable             76%
Number winning trades         19     Number losing trades            6

Largest winning trade   $4,850.00    Largest losing trade    $-2,000.00
Average winning trade   $1,762.50    Average losing trade    $-2,000.00
Ratio avg win/avg loss       0.88    Avg trade (win & loss)     $859.50

Max consecutive winners        6     Max consecutive losers          2
Avg # bars in winners          2     Avg # bars in losers            6

Max closed-out drawdown $-4,000.00   Max intra-day drawdown  $-4,775.00
Profit factor                2.79    Max # of contracts held         1
Account size required   $7,775.00    Return on account             276%
```

Figure 6.9 Another smash day pattern example

```
Data           : DAY T-BONDS        67/99
Calc Dates     : 01/26/89 - 08/27/98

Num. Conv. P. Value  Comm  Slippage  Margin  Format  Drive:\Path\FileName
--------------------------------------------------------------------------
 144  -3  $ 31.250  $ 55  $   0   $ 3,000  CSI     C:\GD\BACK67\F061.DTA

/////////////////////////////// ALL TRADES  - Test 4 \\\\\\\\\\\\\\\\\\\\\\\\\\\\

Total net profit        $13,303.75
Gross profit            $18,000.00    Gross loss              $-4,696.25

Total # of trades               28    Percent profitable            89%
Number winning trades           25    Number losing trades           3

Largest winning trade    $2,413.75    Largest losing trade    $-1,586.25
Average winning trade      $720.00    Average losing trade    $-1,565.42
Ratio avg win/avg loss        0.45    Avg trade (win & loss)     $475.13

Max consecutive winners          9    Max consecutive losers          1
Avg # bars in winners            3    Avg # bars in losers            6

Max closed-out drawdown  $-1,586.25   Max intra-day drawdown  $-2,648.75
Profit factor                  3.83   Max # of contracts held         1
Account size required    $5,648.75    Return on account            235%
```

Figure 6.10 A hidden smash day buy

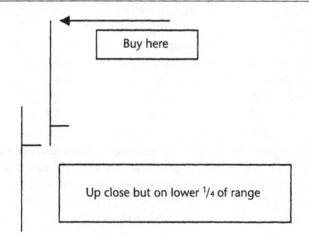

Figure 6.11   A hidden smash day sell

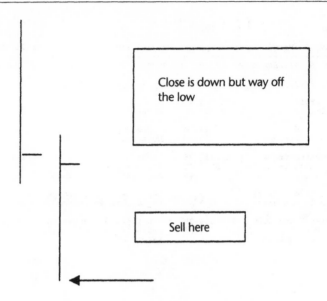

Close is down but way off
the low

Sell here

below the high. The buyers got smashed, in either pattern, and chartists will now come in looking for the kill.

Only to be killed themselves—if the next day—price rallies back and takes out this smash day high. Again we see the pattern of a market failure immediately reversed *the very next day*. This is a most bullish set of events and calls for going long—if the stage has been set for a rally by our background tools such as TDW, TDM, THD, market relationships, overbought/oversold, and trend.

A hidden smash day sell is just the opposite. Look for a down close that is in the upper 25 percent of the day's range and above the open of the day. Our entry comes when price falls below the hidden smash day's low *the very next day* indicating the rally has failed. A quick look at Figure 6.11 should establish what this pattern looks like.

How to Use Smash Day Patterns

There are two ways to use these patterns. Let's first look at the pattern in sharp up- and downtrends—trends you wish you were in or where you want to add a position. In such tight trend up moves, the appearance of a smash down day, hidden or not, sets up our buy for the following day and is precise evidence the trend is intact and ready for traders to have another go at it, another race to the sun.

In a downtrend, the reverse situation will be found to produce excellent indications of when to get back aboard the decline. Here you will be looking for either the naked up close day or a down day that closes in the top of its range. If the very next day prices smash below that day's low, it is time to get short. The examples shown here should help you understand the importance of this technique.

The other way I like to use these smash day setups is to look for a market that has been in a choppy trading range. I then note a smash day and act accordingly once the high or low of the smash

Figure 6.12   Comex silver (daily bars). Graphed by the "Navigator" (Genesis Financial Data Services)

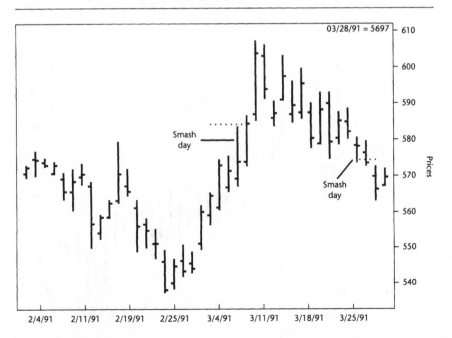

day is penetrated. My thinking is that we will probably see a breakout of the congestion if the smash day is immediately reversed. Such action is suggestive of a market that moved to where all the stops were, and elected all the "breakout babies" who had orders there. The breakout is a magnet for the public to take action and they do. What kills them is the immediate reversal the very next day. They cannot believe their "luck" and decide to hold on despite the reversal; a few days later, they pitch their positions adding fuel to the move we hooked up with thanks to the smash day pattern.

Confucius must have been a chartist when he said that one picture (one chart) is worth a thousand words. I have marked off examples of the smash day pattern in trading ranges for your study. These appear as Figures 6.12 through 6.17.

Figure 6.13   Day T-bonds (daily bars). Graphed by the "Navigator" (Genesis Financial Data Services)

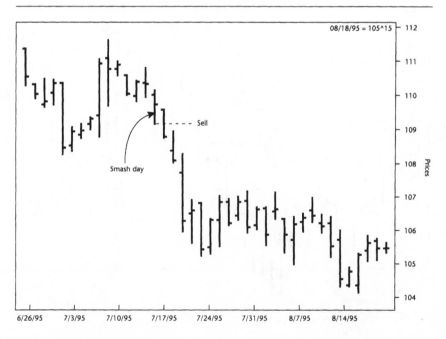

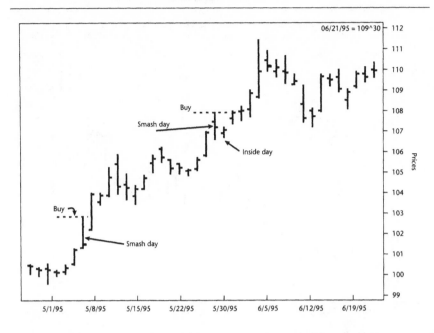

Figure 6.14   Day T-bonds (daily bars). Graphed by the "Navigator" (Genesis Financial Data Services)

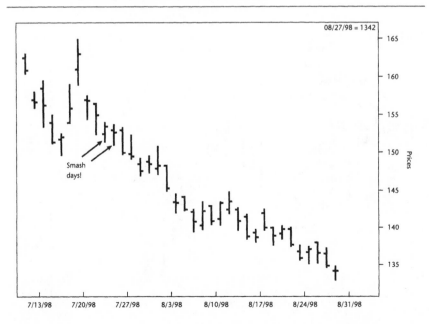

Figure 6.15   Soybean meal (daily bars). Graphed by the "Navigator" (Genesis Financial Data Services)

Figure 6.16   Comex silver (daily bars). Graphed by the "Navigator" (Genesis Financial Data Services)

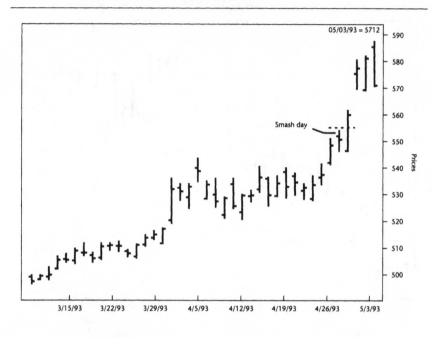

Figure 6.17   CBT wheat (daily bars). Graphed by the "Navigator" (Genesis Financial Data Services)

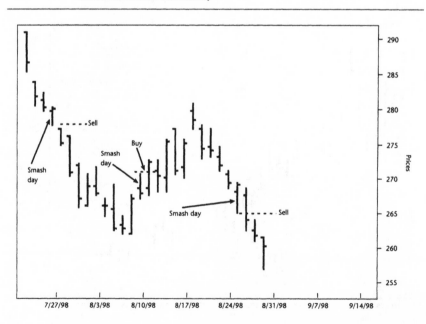

Specialists' Trap

Here is a pattern that uses the smash day idea in yet another fashion. This idea comes from Richard Wyckoff who authored a course on stock trading in the 1930s. I have affinity for Wyckoff's work because, in 1966 and 1967, I worked right across from the library in Carmel, California, where Wyckoff wrote much of the material that in later years he donated to the library. As fate would have it, I stumbled on his donation on my lunch hour one day and thereafter broke bread with his writings for the next year.

The Wyckoff concept is that markets are "manipulated" perhaps not by a manipulator, as you would think, but more by a collective consciousness, the great anamorphic "them" or "they." This group of "them," Wyckoff teaches, moves the market to draw the public into the game at the wrong times. The specialists on the floor of the New York Stock Exchange, who keep book on stocks, have often been accused of "running" and rigging prices to trap the public, hence my term "specialists' trap," but I do not assign any manipulation to them, only to a much more cosmic notion of price movement. I know specialists: One, Bill Abhrams, has been a friend for 15 years and has convincingly proven to me they do not rig stock prices.

The selling "trap" consists of a nice uptrending market that moves sideways in a box or congestion for 5 to 10 days, then breaks out to the upside with a naked close above the entire trading range. The true low of the breakout day then becomes a critical point. If it is broken below, or taken out in the next 1 to 3 days, there is a great probability the upside breakout was false and the public bought a bill of goods. They were trapped into an emotional buy, and the distributors of stocks or commodities most likely unloaded, on strength, to the masses.

A specialists' buy trap is just the opposite. Look for a downtrending market that stabilizes sideways for 5 to 10 days, then breaks out to the downside, with a naked close lower than all the daily lows of the trading range. In theory, you would think this would plummet prices much lower. The truth is it usually does. But, if a snapback takes place, lifting price above the true high of the break day, a market reversal has most likely occurred. All the sell stops below the market were triggered; the public started the breakdown and is now afraid to buy the trend reversal.

I am showing a few actual examples for your observation (Figures 6.18–6.25). The last chart is that of Exxon, a stock.

Figure 6.18 Comex gold (daily bars). Graphed by the "Navigator" (Genesis Financial Data Services)

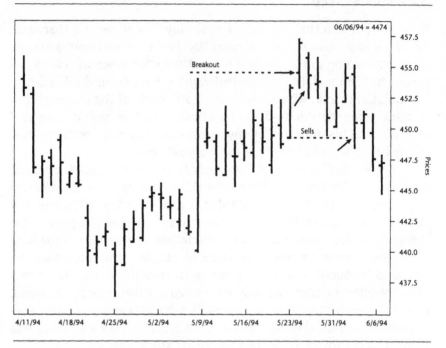

Figure 6.19 Comex gold (daily bars). Graphed by the "Navigator" (Genesis Financial Data Services)

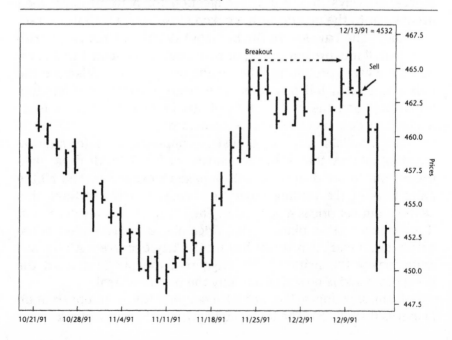

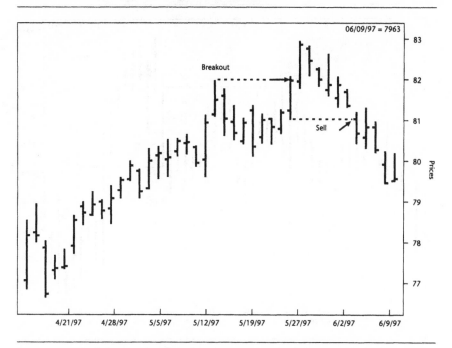

Figure 6.20 Feeder cattle (daily bars). Graphed by the "Navigator" (Genesis Financial Data Services)

Figure 6.21 Cotton #2 (daily bars). Graphed by the "Navigator" (Genesis Financial Data Services)

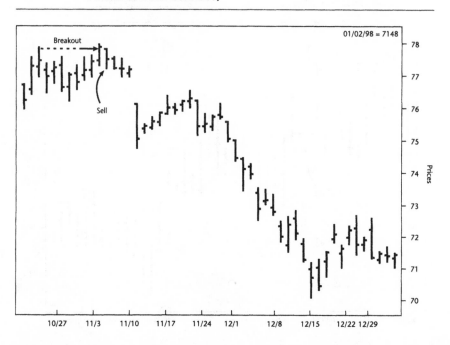

Figure 6.22 Cotton #2 (daily bars). Graphed by the "Navigator" (Genesis Financial Data Services)

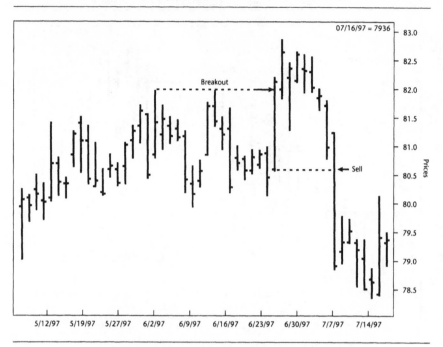

Figure 6.23 New York Light (daily bars). Graphed by the "Navigator" (Genesis Financial Data Services)

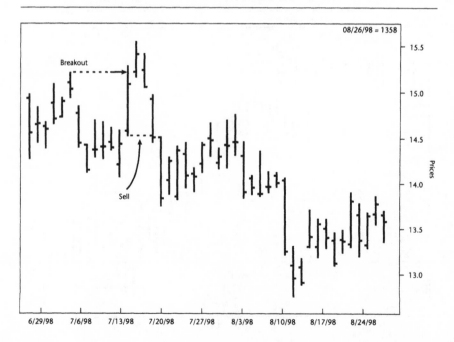

Figure 6.24 Cocoa (daily bars). Graphed by the "Navigator" (Genesis Financial Data Services)

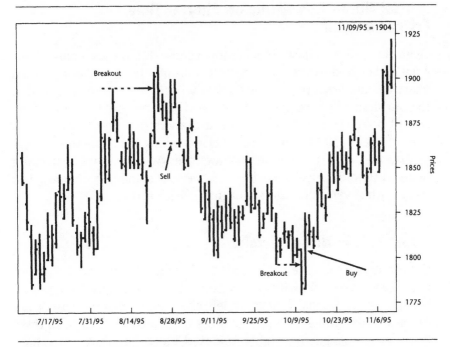

Figure 6.25 XON: Exxon Corporation (daily bars). Graphed by the "Navigator" (Genesis Financial Data Services)

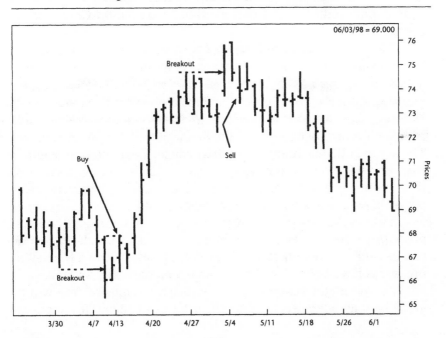

A Vital Note—This Works on Shorter Time Frames as Well

Over the years, I have seen many successful trades using these smash day and traps on 5-minute, 30-minute, and hourly price charts of market activity. Day traders will certainly want to add this to your arsenal of trading techniques. These patterns represent excellent points of entry for short-term traders. The key, though, is to make certain you have something else backing the trade that is suggestive of the action you are taking; otherwise you are just using price to predict price. Your best trades will come from loading the trade with several qualifiers, not just a price structure.

Oops! This Is Not a Mistake

If there is any mistake to the pattern I am about to reveal, it is my mistake to go public with this pattern. It is the most reliable of all short-term patterns I have researched and traded. Numerous other authors and system developers have incorporated it in their work. A few (e.g., the highly talented Linda Bradford Ratschke; Bruce Babcock, the critic's critic; and Jake Bernstein) have been honorable enough to give me credit, whereas many more fail to or even claim credit for this pattern that I first taught to my followers in 1978.

The pattern is based on an overemotional response, then a quick reversal of the concomitant overreaction of price. The overreaction is a large gap in price from last night's close to the next morning's opening. The precise overreaction we are looking for to give us a buy signal *is an opening that is below the previous day's low.* Such a rare occurrence indicates a potential market reversal. The setup is the extreme selling that causes people to panic with a rush of selling as price opens, so much so that price opens less than the prior day's range. This is a most unusual occurrence as price almost always opens within the prior day's range.

That is the setup. The entry comes when, following the lower open, price then rallies back to the previous day's low. If the market can muster up enough strength to do that, most likely, the selling pressures have been abated and a sharp market rally will follow.

As you might suspect, a sell is just the opposite. You will be looking for an open greater than the prior day's high. The emotional response or setup is a huge amount of buying right on the open that causes a large gap, driving price above the prior high. Our entry then comes from price falling back to the prior high, telling us the gap could not hold, giving us a strong short-term suggestion of lower prices to come.

The name Oops! comes from the price action as the public pitches their positions and sells short on the opening based on news, charts, and the like. For a moment, they appear to be on the right track; but about the time price rallies back to the prior day's low, their broker calls to tell them price is moving against them usually saying something like, "Oops! We may have done the wrong thing [again], price is coming back pretty strong. Do you want to stay short?"

By the time the collective public makes up their mind to now get out of the losing trade, price is above yesterday's low and their new buying or short covering adds momentum to the rally we positioned ourselves for. Figures 6.26 and 6.27 show how the Oops! signals will appear.

Okay, now let's see how we might use this pattern. We can start with taking buy signals in the S&P 500 on any day of the week except

---

Figure 6.26 The Oops! buy signal

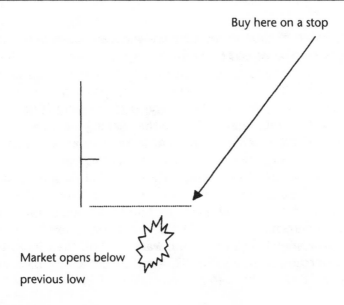

Buy here on a stop

Market opens below

previous low

Figure 6.27   The Oops! sell signal

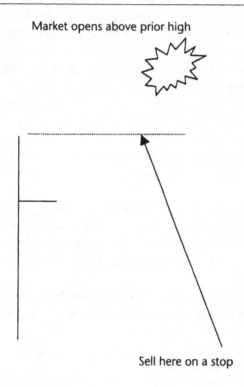

Market opens above prior high

Sell here on a stop

Wednesday or Thursday, the days we know are most apt to lead to declines (see Figure 6.28). The results speak more loudly than anything I might say about this pattern: The 82 percent plus accuracy, $42,687 of profits, and a very large average profit per trade of $438 are quite remarkable considering the trade usually lasts 1½ days. That is, we buy today and are out on the opening tomorrow. The stop was a flat $2,000 loss. You may want to read about stops and exits (Chapter 10) to improve on what I am presenting here.

How about the Bond market? Here we will take long trades any day of the week except Wednesday and a stop loss of $1,800 from the point of entry. Our exit is the bailout technique, soon to be discussed. As shown in Figure 6.29, the results here sure blow the random walk academicians out of the water and off their ivory towers with 86 percent accuracy, $27,875 profits, and a very nice average profit per trade of $201, after commissions of $50.

Figure 6.28 The Oops! pattern at work

```
Data           : S&P 500 IND-9967    09/80
Calc Dates     : 09/15/87 - 08/28/98

Num. Conv. P. Value  Comm  Slippage  Margin  Format  Drive:\Path\FileName
--------------------------------------------------------------------------
 149    2   $  2.500  $ 0    $  0    $ 3,000  CT/PC   C:\GD\BACK67MS\F59.DAT

/////////////////////////////// ALL TRADES  - Test 1 \\\\\\\\\\\\\\\\\\\\\\\\\\\\\\

Total net profit         $42,687.50
Gross profit             $76,687.50    Gross loss                 $-34,000.00

Total # of trades                98    Percent profitable                 82%
Number winning trades            81    Number losing trades                17

Largest winning trade     $3,950.00    Largest losing trade        $-2,000.00
Average winning trade       $946.76    Average losing trade        $-2,000.00
Ratio avg win/avg loss         0.47    Avg trade (win & loss)         $435.59

Max consecutive winners          23    Max consecutive losers               3
Avg # bars in winners             1    Avg # bars in losers                 1

Max closed-out drawdown  $-6,000.00    Max intra-day drawdown      $-6,000.00
Profit factor                  2.25    Max # of contracts held              1
Account size required     $9,000.00    Return on account                 474%
```

On the sell side, the rules are to sell on Wednesday if our Oops! opening gap and failure occur. Since 1990, there have been 55 trades with 31 winners netting $9,875 using a closer $1,000 stop and 4-day bailout exit. In the S&Ps, the best day to sell has been Thursday, which shows 78 percent winners and $14,200 of profits.

Figure 6.29 Using Oops! on bond trades

```
Data           : DAY T-BONDS-9967    01/80
Calc Dates     : 01/01/90 - 08/28/98

Num. Conv. P. Value  Comm  Slippage  Margin  Format  Drive:\Path\FileName
--------------------------------------------------------------------------
  44   -5   $ 31.250  $ 0    $  0    $ 3,000  CT/PC   C:\GD\BACK67MS\F62.DAT

/////////////////////////////// ALL TRADES  - Test 1 \\\\\\\\\\\\\\\\\\\\\\\\\\\\\\

Total net profit         $27,875.00
Gross profit             $60,812.50    Gross loss                 $-32,937.50

Total # of trades               138    Percent profitable                 86%
Number winning trades           120    Number losing trades                18

Largest winning trade     $2,031.25    Largest losing trade        $-2,125.00
Average winning trade       $506.77    Average losing trade        $-1,829.86
Ratio avg win/avg loss         0.27    Avg trade (win & loss)         $201.99

Max consecutive winners          24    Max consecutive losers               3
Avg # bars in winners             2    Avg # bars in losers                 3

Max closed-out drawdown  $-5,812.50    Max intra-day drawdown      $-5,812.50
Profit factor                  1.84    Max # of contracts held              1
Account size required     $8,812.50    Return on account                 316%
```

Figure 6.30   The results of the Oops! technique

```
Data          : DAY T-BONDS-9967    01/80
Calc Dates    : 01/01/90 - 08/28/98

Num. Conv. P. Value  Comm Slippage Margin  Format  Drive:\Path\FileName
----------------------------------------------------------------------------
 44   -5  $  31.250  $  0   $  0   $ 3,000  CT/PC   C:\GD\BACK67MS\F62.DAT

///////////////////////////// ALL TRADES  - Test 1 \\\\\\\\\\\\\\\\\\\\\\\\\\\\\

Total net profit          $9,875.00
Gross profit             $34,031.25    Gross loss              $-24,156.25

Total # of trades               55    Percent profitable              56%
Number winning trades           31    Number losing trades            24

Largest winning trade    $2,687.50    Largest losing trade     $-1,093.75
Average winning trade    $1,097.78    Average losing trade     $-1,006.51
Ratio avg win/avg loss        1.09    Avg trade (win & loss)      $179.55

Max consecutive winners          5    Max consecutive losers           3
Avg # bars in winners            4    Avg # bars in losers             3

Max closed-out drawdown  $-4,437.50   Max intra-day drawdown   $-4,437.50
Profit factor                 1.40    Max # of contracts held          1
Account size required    $7,437.50    Return on account              132%
```

Check out the results as shown here to solidify the value of this technique (Figures 6.30 and 6.31).

The most value will come, not from a mechanical rote approach to trading, but from using this technique with some intelligence or layered on top of a setup market. Here is one such example of this

---

Figure 6.31   More results with the Oops! technique

```
Data          : S&P 500 IND-9967    09/80
Calc Dates    : 09/15/87 - 08/28/98

Num. Conv. P. Value  Comm Slippage Margin  Format  Drive:\Path\FileName
----------------------------------------------------------------------------
149    2  $   2.500  $  0   $  0   $ 3,000  CT/PC   C:\GD\BACK67MS\F59.DAT

///////////////////////////// ALL TRADES  - Test 1 \\\\\\\\\\\\\\\\\\\\\\\\\\\\\

Total net profit         $14,200.00
Gross profit             $40,200.00    Gross loss              $-26,000.00

Total # of trades               60    Percent profitable              78%
Number winning trades           47    Number losing trades            13

Largest winning trade    $4,612.50    Largest losing trade     $-2,000.00
Average winning trade      $855.32    Average losing trade     $-2,000.00
Ratio avg win/avg loss        0.42    Avg trade (win & loss)      $236.67

Max consecutive winners         14    Max consecutive losers           2
Avg # bars in winners            2    Avg # bars in losers             2

Max closed-out drawdown  $-6,725.00   Max intra-day drawdown   $-7,012.50
Profit factor                 1.54    Max # of contracts held          1
Account size required   $10,012.50    Return on account              141%
```

Figure 6.32 Buying on any day but Thursday with the Oops! technique

```
Data            : DAY T-BONDS-9967    01/80
Calc Dates      : 01/01/90 - 08/28/98

Num. Conv. P. Value  Comm  Slippage  Margin  Format  Drive:\Path\FileName
------------------------------------------------------------------------
  44   -5  $  31.250  $  0  $  0  $  3,000  CT/PC   C:\GD\BACK67MS\F62.DAT

///////////////////////////// ALL TRADES  - Test 3 \\\\\\\\\\\\\\\\\\\\\\\\\\\
```

Total net profit	$24,625.00		
Gross profit	$46,750.00	Gross loss	$-22,125.00
Total # of trades	66	Percent profitable	81%
Number winning trades	54	Number losing trades	12
Largest winning trade	$2,625.00	Largest losing trade	$-2,125.00
Average winning trade	$865.74	Average losing trade	$-1,843.75
Ratio avg win/avg loss	0.46	Avg trade (win & loss)	$373.11
Max consecutive winners	20	Max consecutive losers	2
Avg # bars in winners	3	Avg # bars in losers	6
Max closed-out drawdown	$-5,500.00	Max intra-day drawdown	$-5,500.00
Profit factor	2.11	Max # of contracts held	1
Account size required	$8,500.00	Return on account	289%

type of thinking. The results in Figure 6.32 are derived from taking my Oops! buy signals in the Bonds on any day but Thursday if Friday's 9-day moving average is less than Thursday's. The entry is Oops! as taught. The exit is the close on the first profitable opening after 3 days in the trade: 81 percent of these trades made money,

Figure 6.33 Oops! sells on Wednesday

```
Data            : DAY T-BONDS-9967    01/80
Calc Dates      : 01/01/90 - 08/28/98

Num. Conv. P. Value  Comm  Slippage  Margin  Format  Drive:\Path\FileName
------------------------------------------------------------------------
  44   -5  $  31.250  $  0  $  0  $  3,000  CT/PC   C:\GD\BACK67MS\F62.DAT

///////////////////////////// ALL TRADES  - Test 4 \\\\\\\\\\\\\\\\\\\\\\\\\\\
```

Total net profit	$13,406.25		
Gross profit	$25,281.25	Gross loss	$-11,875.00
Total # of trades	34	Percent profitable	79%
Number winning trades	27	Number losing trades	7
Largest winning trade	$2,375.00	Largest losing trade	$-1,812.50
Average winning trade	$936.34	Average losing trade	$-1,696.43
Ratio avg win/avg loss	0.55	Avg trade (win & loss)	$394.30
Max consecutive winners	8	Max consecutive losers	1
Avg # bars in winners	4	Avg # bars in losers	6
Max closed-out drawdown	$-2,781.25	Max intra-day drawdown	$-3,312.50
Profit factor	2.12	Max # of contracts held	1
Account size required	$6,312.50	Return on account	212%

$24,625, in fact. Check out the high average profit per trade of $373. On the sell side, the results reflect taking Oops! sell signals on Wednesday if the 9-day average is greater on Tuesday than Monday, which reflects an overbought market. These signals have been 79 percent accurate netting $13,406, and a surprising $394 profit per trade—not bad for a short-term trade, using the same rules as above for stop and exit as on the long trade (see Figure 6.33).

S&P Oops! Trading

The same idea meets with success in trading the S&P; here the best buy days, given the oversold criteria as established by the 9-day trend, are Tuesday, Wednesday, and Friday. This combination shows 81 percent accuracy and $22,650 of profits with an average profit, after losses, of $456, a remarkable feat for getting in and out the same day (see Figure 6.34). The idea of the 9-day moving average to set up the trade is based on work by Joe Krutsinger, a protégé of mine and avid system developer.

The best sell in this market, using the 9-day overbought technique is to take sells on Wednesday to make $18,962 with 89 percent accuracy on 35 trades (see Figure 6.35). The average profit of $486 per trade drives home the validity of the approach.

Figure 6.34   Oops! buys in a downtrend on Tuesday, Wednesday, and Friday

```
Data            : S&P 500 IND-9967      09/80
Calc Dates      : 09/15/87 - 08/28/98

Num. Conv. P. Value  Comm  Slippage  Margin  Format  Drive:\Path\FileName
----------------------------------------------------------------------------
149   2  $   2.500  $  0   $   0   $  3,000  CT/PC   C:\GD\BACK67MS\F59.DAT

/////////////////////////////// ALL TRADES  - Test 1 \\\\\\\\\\\\\\\\\\\\\\\\\\\\

Total net profit        $22,362.50
Gross profit            $40,600.00   Gross loss              $-18,237.50

Total # of trades             49     Percent profitable            81%
Number winning trades         40     Number losing trades            9

Largest winning trade    $3,875.00   Largest losing trade     $-2,237.50
Average winning trade    $1,015.00   Average losing trade     $-2,026.39
Ratio avg win/avg loss        0.50   Avg trade (win & loss)      $456.38

Max consecutive winners       28     Max consecutive losers          2
Avg # bars in winners          1     Avg # bars in losers            0

Max closed-out drawdown  $-4,925.00  Max intra-day drawdown   $-4,925.00
Profit factor                 2.22   Max # of contracts held         1
Account size required    $7,925.00   Return on account             282%
```

Figure 6.35 Oops! after the 17th trading day of the month

```
Data          : S&P 500 IND-9967    09/80
Calc Dates    : 09/15/87 - 08/28/98

Num. Conv. P. Value  Comm  Slippage  Margin  Format  Drive:\Path\FileName
-----------------------------------------------------------------------------
 149    2  $  2.500  $  0   $  0    $ 3,000  CT/PC  C:\GD\BACK67MS\F59.DAT

/////////////////////////////// ALL TRADES  - Test 2 \\\\\\\\\\\\\\\\\\\\\\\\\\\\\

Total net profit        $18,962.50
Gross profit            $26,962.50    Gross loss             $-8,000.00

Total # of trades              39    Percent profitable            89%
Number winning trades          35    Number losing trades            4

Largest winning trade   $3,175.00    Largest losing trade    $-2,000.00
Average winning trade     $770.36    Average losing trade    $-2,000.00
Ratio avg win/avg loss       0.38    Avg trade (win & loss)     $486.22

Max consecutive winners        26    Max consecutive losers          2
Avg # bars in winners           1    Avg # bars in losers            2

Max closed-out drawdown $-4,000.00   Max intra-day drawdown  $-4,000.00
Profit factor                3.37    Max # of contracts held         1
Account size required   $7,000.00    Return on account            270%
```

Now let's look at another way of using our Oops! entries in the S&P 500. For years, researchers have noted that stock prices tend to rally around the first of the month. This sets up a perfect Oops! trade. Should this pattern occur at the end of the month, and trading day after the 17th trading day of the month, our pattern and the monthly influence come together. These are good trades!

Knowing this end-of-the-month rally spills into the next month, I tested taking all Oops! in Bonds after the first TDM through the 5th. The results are equally impressive. This combination setup is one of the most powerful short-term trades you will find to consistently appear, month in and month out.

Some observers may suggest we are curve-fitting things here by taking the Oops! signals only during a limited window of opportunity. That could be, but let me hastily add I first became aware of this "window of opportunity" in 1962 when I read Art Merrill's classic, *The Behavior of Prices on Wall Street.* I believe Merrill, a delightful, white-haired grandfather figure, was the first to note the rally tendency at this time and fully discussed it in his works.

All I have done is add my Oops! entry, a reasonable stop and exit, to a known market bias. To the best of my knowledge, no one noticed this same pattern or tendency exists in Bonds until 1988 when I revealed it to my students; so again, we have lots of out-of-sample experience. This is not a conclusion looking for a promise.

Merrill and others, notably Norm Fosback and Glen Parker, have suggested the end-of-the-month stock rally is due to mutual funds balancing and window-dressing their holdings. Once I discovered that Bonds rally at this time, I took the position that stocks rally not because of the funds but because of Bonds. As go Bonds, so go stocks. Always keep in mind Bonds (interest rates) are the dogs wagging the tail, which is stocks.

Virtually any time you have a bullish outlook or bias in the market, Oops! buys are worth taking, just as Oops! sells are worth taking when you have a bearish outlook. This pattern works wonders, given an underlying reason. It is the single best pattern I have discovered; enjoy it, treat it with care, use it with wisdom.

chapter 7

separating the buyers from the sellers

Which came first, the chicken or the egg, the buyer or the seller? I suppose this is the ultimate Zen koan that speculators must answer before attaining enlightenment. On the surface, it seems prices should never vary much if you must have a seller to give shares or contracts to a buyer. Shouldn't they balance each other out?

In a perfect world they would, but this is an imperfect world and an even more imperfect game of chance. Reality, as read in your daily newspaper or spoken in quotes from your broker, tells us prices do move, often wildly. The reason for price changes is not the amount of shares or contracts bought and sold; after all, they are matched. The reason price fluctuates is that one side, the buyer or the seller, blinks.

In other words, one side in this equation wants to establish a position and will pay up, or sell down. The imbalance that causes price change is not one of volume but of immediacy . . . the side that wants it and wants it now, is the side that pushes prices higher or lower.

As mentioned, we can break down the amount of buying and selling that took place in a given day by using the opening price. This chapter describes the elements of a trading system and approach I used to make more than $1,000,000 in 1987.

Consider this: Each day the commodity opens for trading at a price established by an open outcry based on the buy and sell orders that have built up overnight.

On March 27, 1998, May Bellies opened at 46.20, traded down to a low at 45.95 and up to a high at 48.60. Buyers were able to "push" prices 2.40 points above the open and .25 points below the opening. We have two swings here, the upswing of 2.40 points and a downswing of .25. Price closed for the day at 48.32 up from the previous day's close at 46.40.

The following charts show the greatest swing values marked off so you can visually see the actual workings in a real market. Figure 7.1 is of Soybeans in March 1990. Each day you have a buy swing and a sell swing. The direction of the close ± the open tells us which side won the battle. In this case, after the open, a selling wave was established and price went down that .25 in Bellies amount; we then closed higher. If the day after the up close, price moves more than .25 points

Figure 7.1 Soybeans (daily bars). Graphed by the "Navigator" (Genesis Financial Data Services)

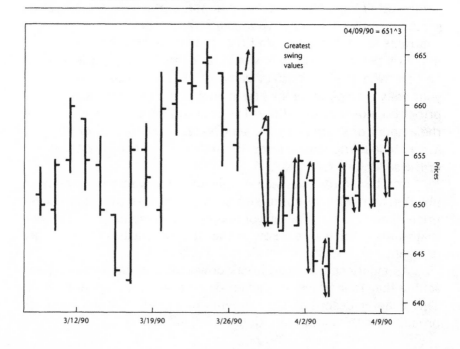

below the opening, we have a new "amount" of sellers in the market-place. Thus a sell signal may be in effect as we have drawn more sellers in today than yesterday.

We can take this a little further. If I add up all the open to low swings for the past few days, I have an average of the amount of selling swings that have taken place and suspect that any swing from today's open that exceeds this average may be indicative of a sell signal.

But hold on, it is a bit more complicated. To really get a handle on the sellers, you need to take this measure on just days that closed above the opening, as this swing value is the amount price could decline *without* triggering a down close day.

By the same token, if you were to add up the swings from the open to the daily highs (on down close days), you would arrive at the swing values the market could rally without setting off a wave of buying resulting in an up close.

Greatest Swing Value

I call this concept "greatest swing value (GSV)." It can be used in many profitable ways. The more work you do with the concept, the more you will appreciate the logic of finding the upswings on down days and downswings on up days. I categorize these swings as "failure swings": The market could swing that much, yet not hold it or follow through, and then closed in the opposite direction.

Let's look at some things you could do with these values. You could determine the average failure swings, say for the past few days, and use that as your entry added or subtracted to the next day's opening. Or how about taking all the failure swings for X number of days and then take one or two standard deviations of that value added to the value to trigger your entry?

I will start with a simple and profitable way of using these values for trading the Bond market. My first step is to create a setup for the trade, as I don't want to trade on just one technical goody all by itself. My setup will be an oversold market: Prices have been declining, so a rally of some sort should be in the future, and I am combining this with one of my prized possessions, the Trade Day of the Week (TDW), as discussed earlier.

In this case, the first part of the setup is to have today's close lower than the close 5 days ago, suggesting Yin may turn into Yang.

Figure 7.2   Greatest swing values in the bonds

```
Data          : DAY T-BONDS-9967    01/80
Calc Dates    : 01/01/90 - 08/28/98

Num. Conv. P. Value  Comm  Slippage  Margin  Format  Drive:\Path\FileName
--------------------------------------------------------------------------
  44   -5  $  31.250  $  0   $  0    $  3,000  CT/PC   C:\GD\BACK67MS\F62.DAT
```

/////////////////////////////// ALL TRADES - Test 1 \\\\\\\\\\\\\\\\\\\\\\\\\\\\\\

Total net profit	$52,812.50		
Gross profit	$105,000.00	Gross loss	$-52,187.50
Total # of trades	161	Percent profitable	75%
Number winning trades	122	Number losing trades	39
Largest winning trade	$3,437.50	Largest losing trade	$-1,718.75
Average winning trade	$860.66	Average losing trade	$-1,338.14
Ratio avg win/avg loss	0.64	Avg trade (win & loss)	$328.03
Max consecutive winners	13	Max consecutive losers	2
Avg # bars in winners	4	Avg # bars in losers	3
Max closed-out drawdown	$-6,343.75	Max intra-day drawdown	$-6,781.25
Profit factor	2.01	Max # of contracts held	1
Account size required	$9,781.25	Return on account	539%

/////////////////////////////// LONG TRADES - Test 1 \\\\\\\\\\\\\\\\\\\\\\\\\\\\\\

Total net profit	$48,187.50		
Gross profit	$88,281.25	Gross loss	$-40,093.75
Total # of trades	122	Percent profitable	77%
Number winning trades	94	Number losing trades	28
Largest winning trade	$3,437.50	Largest losing trade	$-1,687.50
Average winning trade	$939.16	Average losing trade	$-1,431.92
Ratio avg win/avg loss	0.65	Avg trade (win & loss)	$394.98
Max consecutive winners	13	Max consecutive losers	2
Avg # bars in winners	4	Avg # bars in losers	4

/////////////////////////////// SHORT TRADES - Test 1 \\\\\\\\\\\\\\\\\\\\\\\\\\\\\\

Total net profit	$4,625.00		
Gross profit	$16,718.75	Gross loss	$-12,093.75
Total # of trades	39	Percent profitable	71%
Number winning trades	28	Number losing trades	11
Largest winning trade	$1,593.75	Largest losing trade	$-1,718.75
Average winning trade	$597.10	Average losing trade	$-1,099.43
Ratio avg win/avg loss	0.54	Avg trade (win & loss)	$118.59
Max consecutive winners	6	Max consecutive losers	2
Avg # bars in winners	2	Avg # bars in losers	2
Max closed-out drawdown	$-2,500.00	Max intra-day drawdown	$-2,500.00
Profit factor	1.38	Max # of contracts held	1
Account size required	$5,500.00	Return on account	84%

I also want to limit my buying to only one of 3 days of the week; they are Tuesday, Wednesday, and Friday.

Once that part of the setup exists, I will take the difference from open to the high for each of the past 4 days and divide that by 4 to get the average "buy swing." I want real proof the market is tracking in fresh ground, new territory, so I will be a buyer above the opening at an amount equal to 180 percent of the 4-day swing value average.

The *sell signal* is a mirror image in that I take the distance from the open to the low for each of the last 4 days and divide by 4 to get the average. This is also multiplied by 180 percent and subtracted from the opening *if the sell setup exits.*

The sell setup consists of Bonds closing greater than the close 6 days ago, and for even better performance, I would also like to see the price of Gold lower than the price of Gold 20 days ago.

Whether long or short, my stop is $1,600. I will take profits on the first profitable opening after being in the trade for 2 days. The results of this program from 1990 to 1998 are shown in Figure 7.2. As you can see, they are rather remarkable, telling us the importance of setup criteria coupled with the greatest swing value concept. Frankly, I do not know of any Bond systems being sold by all the technical hotshots that can match these results.

Stock Index Trading with Greatest Swing Value

The same basic formula works for trading the S&P 500. Again, we will take 180 percent of the 4-day average buy swing value (the highs minus the opens) and, for sell, the 4-day average swing sell value (closes minus the lows). As you might suspect, the results can be dramatically improved by demanding Bonds close higher than 15 days ago for a buy and lower than 15 days ago for a sell. Fundamentals do make a difference; don't let any frayed cuff chartist or fast-talking technician tell you otherwise. Our TDW filter will be to buy on Monday, Tuesday, or Wednesday. Shorts will be taken any day but Monday. The setup also consists of a close lower than six days ago for a buy, higher than six days ago for a sell, giving us an overextended market condition.

The results say it all, $105,675 of profits with 67 percent winning trades, using a flat dollar stop of $2,500 and the bailout exit (Figure 7.3). Not as much money was made on the short side, but

Figure 7.3 Greatest swing value at .80 in the S&P 500

```
Data        : S&P 500 IND-9967    09/80
Calc Dates  : 09/15/87 - 08/28/98

Num. Conv. P. Value  Comm  Slippage  Margin  Format  Drive:\Path\FileName
-------------------------------------------------------------------------
 149   2  $  2.500  $  0  $  0    $  3,000  CT/PC  C:\GD\BACK67MS\F59.DAT
```

//////////////////////////// ALL TRADES - Test 4 \\\\\\\\\\\\\\\\\\\\\\\\\\\\

Total net profit	$105,675.00		
Gross profit	$277,250.00	Gross loss	-171,575.00
Total # of trades	247	Percent profitable	67%
Number winning trades	167	Number losing trades	80
Largest winning trade	$10,962.50	Largest losing trade	$-3,587.50
Average winning trade	$1,660.18	Average losing trade	$-2,144.69
Ratio avg win/avg loss	0.77	Avg trade (win & loss)	$427.83
Max consecutive winners	10	Max consecutive losers	5
Avg # bars in winners	4	Avg # bars in losers	4
Max closed-out drawdown	$-12,500.00	Max intra-day drawdown	$-13,462.50
Profit factor	1.61	Max # of contracts held	1
Account size required	$16,462.50	Return on account	641%

//////////////////////////// LONG TRADES - Test 4 \\\\\\\\\\\\\\\\\\\\\\\\\\\\

Total net profit	$51,575.00		
Gross profit	$148,437.50	Gross loss	$-96,862.50
Total # of trades	123	Percent profitable	65%
Number winning trades	81	Number losing trades	42
Largest winning trade	$10,962.50	Largest losing trade	$-3,587.50
Average winning trade	$1,832.56	Average losing trade	$-2,306.25
Ratio avg win/avg loss	0.79	Avg trade (win & loss)	$419.31
Max consecutive winners	8	Max consecutive losers	4
Avg # bars in winners	4	Avg # bars in losers	3

//////////////////////////// SHORT TRADES - Test 4 \\\\\\\\\\\\\\\\\\\\\\\\\\\\

Total net profit	$54,100.00		
Gross profit	$128,812.50	Gross loss	$-74,712.50
Total # of trades	124	Percent profitable	69%
Number winning trades	86	Number losing trades	38
Largest winning trade	$9,125.00	Largest losing trade	$-3,100.00
Average winning trade	$1,497.82	Average losing trade	$-1,966.12
Ratio avg win/avg loss	0.76	Avg trade (win & loss)	$436.29
Max consecutive winners	9	Max consecutive losers	6
Avg # bars in winners	4	Avg # bars in losers	6
Max closed-out drawdown	$-16,575.00	Max intra-day drawdown	$-16,662.50
Profit factor	1.72	Max # of contracts held	1
Account size required	$19,662.50	Return on account	275%

money was made; and considering the gargantuan bull market this took place within, the results are pretty good. Proof comes from the average profit per trade of $427.

More Uses for the Concept

I have also used this idea to help me when I am confused. If I am in a position and looking for a place to exit, or maybe want to establish a position but do not have any clear-cut entry points, I will use the GSV to tell me when the current spate of buying/selling has been reversed. All I need to do is calculate the buy and sell swing values running the average as a tight stop or entry point.

Intraday traders can use this value a bit differently. What many want to do is sell what should be an overbought area and buy an oversold area. In this case, the GSV will tell you about how far above the open you can sell, the largest failed value of the past few days; then you would place a stop and reverse slightly above that value. You would buy below the open a distance of the largest failed down swing value, with a stop below that.

Here is a case in point. Table 7.1 shows the daily action of the S&P 500 in March 1998 along with the *sell swing values*. Once we arrive at the 4-day average on March 16 and multiply it by 180 percent, we have a buy point (5.50 points) that much below the opening on the 17th with a fill at 1086.70. Table 7.1 shows how it looked.

Your stop on the long should be 225 percent of the 4-day average swing value of 3.57 or 8.00 – the 1092.20 open giving us a stop at 1084.20.

Table 7.1   Daily action of the S&P 500

	Open	High	Low	Close	GSV (Greatest Swing Value)
3/11	1,078.00	1,082.40	1,077.20	1,080.80	0.80
3/12	1,080.00	1,085.20	1,075.50	1,084.00	4.50
3/13	1,087.00	1,088.60	1,078.40	1,080.90	8.60
3/16	1,085.00	1,092.40	1,084.60	1,091.70	.40

GSV 4 Day Average = 14.30/4 or 3.57 × 180 = 6.45
3/17 Open is 1,092.20 – 6.45 Buy at 1,085.75

	Open	High	Low	Close	
3/17	1,092.20	1,094.50	1,086.00	1,094.20	

You can always determine the general area where a market should find support and resistance with the GSV concept. My work suggests contra trend moves of 180 percent with a 225 percent stop work quite well.

Yet another way I have traded and made money with this idea is to wait for a down close in the S&P 500 on Friday. I then buy Monday at the open plus Friday's high minus Friday's open swing value. I back this with Bonds closing on Friday greater than they did 15 days ago. The following results show simply using the bailout exit and a $2,500 stop. Practically speaking, I exit the trade at the open minus the swing value, unless the swing value is very large. In that case, I admit defeat if price trades below the lowest price seen in the day prior to going long. The time period here is from 1982 through March 1998. This is the most successful interday mechanical trading technique I know of.

This is a strong online trade because once the setup is present (Bonds greater than 15 days ago, and Friday closes down), you buy at the next day's open plus the buying swing value from Friday. Certainly, this takes no great skill, only the willingness to patiently wait for trades, then the gumption to put them on (see Figure 7.4).

**Figure 7.4   Greatest swing value buying on Mondays following a
down close**

```
Data            : S&P 500 IND-9967    09/80
Calc Dates      : 09/15/87 - 08/28/98

 Num. Conv. P. Value  Comm  Slippage  Margin  Format  Drive:\Path\FileName
------------------------------------------------------------------------------
 149   2  $  2.500  $  0   $  0    $  3,000  CT/PC  C:\GD\BACK67MS\F59.DAT

///////////////////////////////// ALL TRADES  - Test 1 \\\\\\\\\\\\\\\\\\\\\\\\\\\\\\\

Total net profit        $57,087.50
Gross profit           $117,587.50    Gross loss            $-60,500.00

Total # of trades            161      Percent profitable           86%
Number winning trades        139      Number losing trades          22

Largest winning trade    $7,625.00    Largest losing trade   $-2,750.00
Average winning trade      $845.95    Average losing trade   $-2,750.00
Ratio avg win/avg loss        0.30    Avg trade (win & loss)    $354.58

Max consecutive winners       26      Max consecutive losers         2
Avg # bars in winners          1      Avg # bars in losers           2

Max closed-out drawdown  $-5,500.00   Max intra-day drawdown $-5,500.00
Profit factor                 1.94    Max # of contracts held        1
Account size required    $8,500.00    Return on account            671%
```

Similar trading strategies can be developed for all markets using the GSV concept; just make certain you first define valid set-ups for the buys and sells. My favorite setups are days of the week, highly correlated data2 streams, seasonals, market patterns, and overbought/sold conditions.

Some Pointers

Over the years, I have tried various time periods to see whether there is any ideal number of days to use in the calculation. My original thought was that one would want to use a 10-day period to arrive at the best average; after all, the more observations of swing value variance the more stable the answer should be, or so I thought. I was wrong on that. In almost all cases, the previous 1 to 4 days produce the best value in trading or developing systems.

The basics here involve volatility breakouts above or below the opening. The amount of breakout we are looking for is the amount that contained moves up to this point. Thus, a critical element is to only take buy signals after down days, sells after up days.

Finally, keep in mind this is a "dumb" technique; it knows not when a big trade will come or even when a winning trade will be delivered on a silver platter. That is why you cannot pick and choose these trades, you must simply take them, one at a time, as they come out of the hopper. If you pick and choose, you will invariably pick the losers and walk away from the winners. It is nothing personal, we all do, and *the way to beat this devil is to take 'em all.*

To my way of thinking, the GSV concept is the most solid and logical approach to volatility breakouts. This failed swing measure has such great merit that I hope someone else, maybe you, will take it past the point I have reached. Perhaps the better answer lies in the standard deviation approach mentioned earlier, perhaps in using the GSV in relationship to the previous day's range. I am really not certain. What I am certain of is that this is one of the most powerful techniques in my bag of tricks and perhaps the most durable. It has served me well since I had the insight into the idea in 1977. Fancy math may improve the results, but it is not necessary to make this work.

chapter 8

attention, day traders

What I have shared with you so far is the general way I trade. I use daily bar charts to set up patterns and relationships that usually spur short-term moves of 2 to 4 days. This is my style; it may not be yours.

People like the idea of day trading as there is no risk of anything happening overnight. This fear is that a large adverse move may take place from today's close to tomorrow's opening. The fear is news, change, and uncontrollable price action. The idea that at the end of the day it is all over—win, lose, or draw—is attractive. There are no anguishing losses to take home and interrupt your sleep. Make no mistake about it, all this is true, but for everything you get in life you give up something in life. What you give up when day trading is an opportunity to catch a large and sustained move, as mentioned earlier.

To most people, the term "day trading" means being glued to a quote screen throughout the market trading day. They envision images of a high-pressure guy or gal with a phone in each ear, screaming something like "Buy Chicago, sell New York." Certainly, this type of trading is hectic, and if you are going to trade this way, you had better make certain you have the temperament required for the job. I will tell you what I think that temperament is, then tell you what my quest for this Holy Grail of commodity trading has revealed.

Day traders need three qualities; intensity, the ability to make intelligent choices, and the capacity to react without any more thinking to the conditions at hand.

If you are the type who *needs time* to make a decision, or freezes, refusing to take action once a decision has been made, this is not your game. Winning at this game requires making instant decisions and immediately reacting; there is no time for pontificating or reconsidering. If you cannot make decisions this way, you will be slaughtered in a matter of months. It is a game of the quick and the dead. If you are not quick, you will be dead. It is as simple as that. Day trading requires the physical ability to instantly pounce on a market and just as instantly reverse the decision you made just a few seconds ago, if that is what conditions dictate.

Following the intraday ebb and flow of prices on a screen, day after day after day, requires the ability to be focused and intense every hour of each trading session. This is not an occupation for daydreamers. If you cannot maintain concentration, you will get hurt; it is forgetting to do what you should do, not being there (physically or mentally) at that one critical minute, 60 seconds, that spells the difference between life and death in your trading. It is not easy work to stay this focused and intense, particularly when your spouse calls to ask you some mundane question about the garden or plumbing at home, or a close friend calls to chat. Do you have the guts to tell them you can't talk now, to hang up on a close friend, to refuse to take calls from your wife or husband? If so, you are qualified for the job, if not, better rethink day trading.

I assure you the instant you get distracted by that phone call is the instant the market will have a major move, catching you off guard. Well, don't say I didn't warn you. Now let's look at the object of this game. You must also be able to change your view of the future in an instant. This is not a career for hardheaded people.

How a Day Trader Makes Money

A day trader has one objective: to catch the current trend of the market. That is it. That is all you should try to do!

It sounds easy, but trust me—it is far from simple, and for two reasons. The first is that trend identification is an art and science unto itself, and more abstract art at that. It is a blend of Picasso and Cézanne with a splash of Chagall tossed in for fun. Second, even if you correctly spot the trend change, your reactive mind may screw things up and blow it for you. This is especially true if you are long with a loss or nominal profit and suddenly get a sell signal.

Do not confuse day trading with your long-term outlook; that is about something happening in the future. Day traders don't—can't—care about the future. Your only concern is being in phase with the current short-term trend. Your mission, should you accept this assignment, is to mimic what the market is doing. If it is up, you should be long, if down, short. Trying to forecast short-term tops and bottoms is a surefire way to rapidly deplete your bankroll. You want to be with the trend; it is your only friend.

Since greed is a stronger emotion than fear, your response will most often be to "hold and hope" which means you bypass the current new trend, holding on to the long position hoping the sell will be wrong when you should have spun on a dime. Dopes hope, winners are spinners.

My point is we are trying to do two very difficult things, beat the identification of trend changes and beat our "brains" by out-smarting ourselves. That is the challenge. My first technique for identifying trend changes comes from the short-term high and low concept. This concept allows us to identify short-term swing points. A trend change from up to down occurs when a short-term high is exceeded on the upside, a short-term trend change from down to up is identified by price going below the most recent short-term low. Figure 8.1 depicts such trend changes in a classic manner, study it well because reality comes next!

Figure 8.1 Classic patterns of trend change

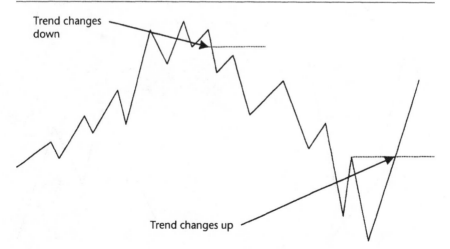

Swing Points as Trend Change Indication

Here are a couple of pointers on this technique. Although the penetration of one of these short-term highs, in a declining market, indicates a trend reversal to the upside, some penetrations are better than others.

There are only two ways a short-term high or low is broken. In an uptrending market, the low that is violated or fallen below will be either a low prior to making a new rally high, as shown at (A) in Figure 8.2, or a low that occurs after decline of a high that then rallies making a lower short-term high; it then declines below the low prior to the rally that failed to make a new high, as shown at (B).

Figure 8.2   Breaking a short-term high or low

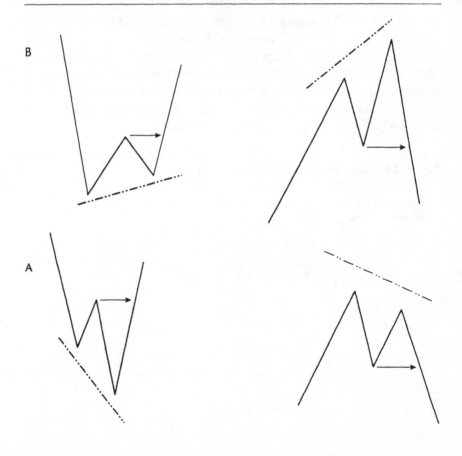

The better indication of a real trend change is the violation of the low shown at (A).

By the same token, a trend reversal to the upside will occur in one of the two following patterns: In (A), the rally peak prior to a new low is violated to the upside, or in (B), the market makes a higher low, then rallies above the short-term high between those two lows. In this case, again, the (A) pattern is the better indication of a real trend reversal.

With that in mind, look at Figure 8.3, which shows a 15-minute bar chart of the September Bonds in 1989. The major trend moves were adequately captured by this technique.

Figure 8.4 again shows Bonds, this time in April 1998, and again you see how the penetration of short-term high and low points enables a trader to be in phase with most of the trend moves for a 10-day time period.

You can use this technique two ways. Some traders may simply buy long and sell short on these changes in trend. That's a basic

Figure 8.3   T-bonds (15-minute bars). Graphed by the "Navigator" (Genesis Financial Data Services)

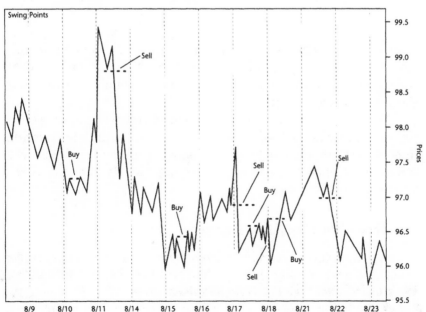

Figure 8.4   T-bonds (15-minute bars). Graphed by the "Navigator" (Genesis Financial Data Services)

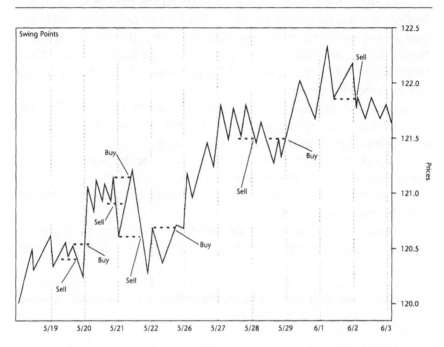

simplistic approach. A more educated attitude would be to take buy/sell signals when confirmed by TDW, TDM, secondary data, and so on, thus filtering our trades with something other than wiggles and waggles on a chart.

Finally, we may use this indication of trend to tell us we can buy on pullbacks, and sell on rallies in unison with the underlying trend. If our indication of trend is positive, and there has been a reversal to the upside, then we can take buy signals from short-term measures or techniques.

The Three-Bar High/Low System

At one point in my career, I had over 30 consecutive winning trades using this next trading strategy. You will first have to calculate a 3-bar moving average of the high and a 3-bar moving average of the lows. (Each bar represents the time period displayed on your chart. Use 5-minute charts for lots of signal, or 15-minute charts if you want a little less hectic trading career.)

The strategy is to buy at the price of the 3-bar moving average of the lows—if the trend is positive, according to the swing point trend identification technique—and take profits at the 3-bar moving average of the highs.

Sell signals are just the opposite. This means you will sell short at the 3-bar moving average of the highs and take profits at the 3-bar moving average of the lows. It is downright foolish to do this unless there is a reason to take only short sales. Our reason might well be that our swing point reversal system has told us the trend is down. Then, and only then, sell the high and cover at the lows.

Now let's try to make some order out of all this. Figure 8.5 shows the addition of the 3-bar moving averages and the swing lines. I have marked the points where trend changes; we switch from buying the lows to shorting the highs following these reversals. The 3-bar high and low entry points are also shown. The game goes like

Figure 8.5   T-bonds (15-minute bars). Graphed by the "Navigator" (Genesis Financial Data Services)

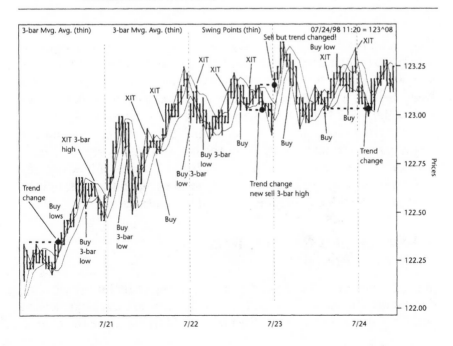

Figure 8.6   T-bonds (15-minute bars). Graphed by the "Navigator" (Genesis Financial Data Services)

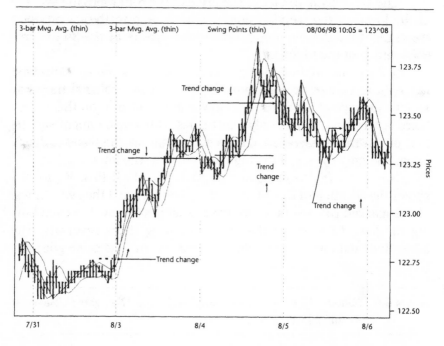

this; trend reversal up so we buy the 3-bar low line and take profits at the 3-bar high and await a pullback to the 3-bar low. If the 3-bar low would create a trend reversal for selling, however, pass on the trade. Sells are just the opposite; await a trend reversal down, then sell all the 3-bar highs and take profits at the 3-bar lows.

Figure 8.6 has all the trend reversals marked off, so you can begin paper trading by looking for the buy and sell entries and exits. I suggest you walk through this chart to get a sense of how one can trade this intraday approach. Note these are 15-minute bars, but the concept will work on 5-minute to 60-minute bars as well.

A New Indicator for Short-Term Traders . . . Will-Spread

Markets move for real reasons, not because of technical whirling dervishes. Things happen in life because there are consequences to actions. Charts do not move the markets. Markets move the charts.

In keeping with that, I also think short-term swings occur because of some external factor. Price never rallies because it is rallying, the rally is the symptom of a cause. Detect that cause and we are several light-years ahead of the average short-term or day trader.

One of my favorite causative indicators is my *Will-Spread* index, a measure of the flow of price between the primary market we are trading and a secondary market that influences the primary. As you know, Bonds influence stocks, and Gold influences Bonds; Will-Spread allows us to spot the inner workings of these market relationships. The index is constructed or calculated by first dividing the price of the market we are trading, the primary market, by the secondary market and multiplying by 100. This creates a spread between the two markets allowing a basic comparison of market interaction.

For day trading on 15-minute bar charts in particular, and most other time frames as well, I then create a 5-period exponential of the spread and subtract that from a 20-period exponential of the spread. By so doing, we can see when one market is heating up over another and get a better sense of these inner-market influences. Granted, this is not a perfect system, but the only perfect approach to day trading I have ever seen are those myriad ads in commodity magazines and newspapers. You can absolutely trust me on this: those are 90 percent hype and 10 percent substance. If anyone really had such an outstanding system, he or she could make 100 times more money trading without the hassle of having to deal with the public. In addition, the tax advantages of trading are gargantuan compared with hawking systems. I have yet to see a totally mechanical day trading system that consistently makes money. Day trading is an art form that must be based on good concepts to be successful.

An Actual Example

Figure 8.7 shows a 30-minute bar chart of the June 1998 Treasury Bonds. Will-Spread, based on the spread between Gold and Bonds, is the index at the bottom of the chart. Our trading strategy should be to look for market rallies whenever this index moves from negative territory, below the zero line, to above it into positive land. A sell is just the opposite; when the index has been positive and then falls below the zero line, it is probably time to sell.

I do not use this index as a be-all, know-all system. I use it as a tool to keep me in correct alignment with the true trend of the market

Figure 8.7   T-bonds (30-minute bars). Graphed by the "Navigator" (Genesis Financial Data Services)

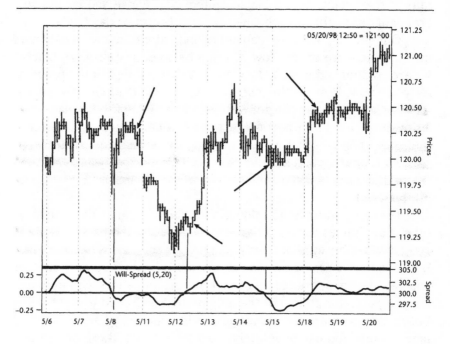

I am trading. In this case, we are looking at Bonds versus Gold. Once price goes from being negative to positive, I will most always wait for one more thing to happen:

> I want the very next trading bar to rally above the high of the bar that switched the index from negative to positive.
>
> I am looking for final confirmation that the trend is still alive.

I am not nearly as comfortable without this confirmation taking place. An exception can be made if other technical gauges such as trendlines or positive oscillator readings are appearing on your chart or screen. You can take such trades, but there is no better proof of a market's ability to rally than taking out the high or falling below the low when a crossing from positive to negative has taken place.

Let's start with the May 8, 1998 chart. The first 30-minute bar saw a big down move resulting in a negative crossing, but the following bar did not fall below that bar's low, so no entry. Finally on the 13:50 bar, we would have sold short as the index was negative and we traded below the prior bar's low. Our entry would have been 120⁷⁄₃₂.

Will-Spread stays negative all that day as well as the next, finally turning positive on May 12 on the 9:50 bar. Now comes the acid test . . . will the rally continue? And it does as the 10:20 bar trades at 119¹⁵⁄₃₂ netting us a gain of 25 ticks or $750 per contract.

We are now long at 119¹⁵⁄₃₂ and looking for a negative crossing to go short. The first break below zero occurs on May 14 on the 12:50 bar. Again, we wait for confirmation, but none comes on the next bar. We now wait for that bar's low to be violated. Our "trailing" stop to exit and reverse is finally elected when the 14:20 bar trades down to 120⁵⁄₃₂. Our net gain is 20 ticks or just a little over $600 per contract.

We steel our nerves for the short trade and await a new development, a penetration of Will-Spread back into the positive zone. This does not take place until the 8:50 bar on May 18. The rally continues with a full-fledged buy at 120¹⁵⁄₃₂ on that day. We lost money on the short, in fact, our net loss was 10 ticks or $312.50.

Could we have prevented this loss? Sure, in retrospect as Monday morning quarterbacks, but blindly following the rules, you would have taken the hit. When this happens, and it most certainly will, I take consolation in the following statement:

Casinos do not win on every roll of the dice either.

We did end the day with a 5-tick profit or about $150 to help lick our wounds and offset the loss, and the next trade (remember, traders fight wars not battles) would have made $500 per contract.

An astute trader may have exited the short position on the second bar of trading when it took out the previous bar's high. Reasons? Will-Spread was quickly approaching the zero line. We should limit losses, and price had a volatility breakout at 120⁵⁄₃₂ for a net loss of just 1 tick or $32.50 plus commissions. You may not have chosen to exit, but that would have been my choice on the strength of the action of Will-Spread in conjunction with the breakout of the trading range. As I said, this is a thinking person's business. If you were in a quandary about what to do, you could have looked at a

5- or 15-minute chart on May 18. There you would have noticed both time frames giving a clear-cut penetration of Will-Spread to the upside suggesting the best course of action would have been—at the very least—to pitch your short position.

Will-Spread and the S&P 500 Stock Index

This same idea works quite well in helping us catch short-term swings in the various stock index contracts such as the New York Stock Exchange, Dow Jones, Value Line, the Mini S&P as well as the S&P 500 full-size contract.

Although Gold makes the world of Bonds go around, it does not have as strong an impact on stocks. As you now know, however, interest rates do; so I suggest you use either T-Bills or Bonds in your Will-Spread setup. Using 30-minute bar charts, I am employing the difference between a 3-period and 15-period exponential average. Admittedly, this is a lot of work to do by hand, but the better quote software such as Omega's Trade Station and Genesis Data have now built my indicator into their programs.

Instead of just randomly choosing time periods to present to you to illustrate the value of Will-Spread, I am first going to show you "The Anatomy of a Crash," by highlighting the biggest crash of all times, the 1987 debacle, as well as the 1997 and 1998 waterfall slides.

The Crash of 1987

Here it is in all its glory; the largest stock market decline in the history of the world! A decline that changed lives and fortunes, a decline of such disastrous proportions lawyers were still suing for damages from the drop 5 years later. Even now, books are written claiming to know why it took place or explain it away. Academics have suggested many ways to prevent the damages of such speculative busts in the future. Big deal, I say; it was predictable—then—not now, with Will-Spread (see Figure 8.8). This amazing index dipped into the negative zone on October 14 at 311.50 staying short all the way through the debacle telling its followers the bottom was not yet in sight. Interest rates vis-à-vis T-Bills were not supportive of the market and without that confirmation we should not look for any buy signals. Indeed, just about any buying, other than the absolute low, would have proven costly.

Figure 8.8 S&P 500 Index (30-minute bars). Graphed by the "Na⌐ ⌐ (Genesis Financial Data Services)

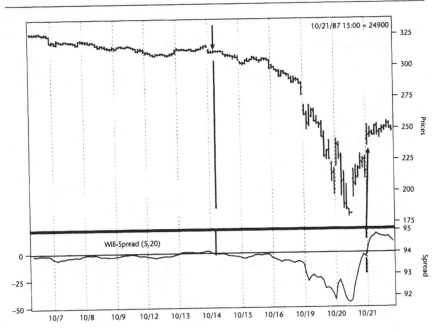

The exit or first crossing back into positive territory came on October 20, 1987, with the S&P bloodied and battered at 219.50, a profit of $46,000 per contract. The margin at the time was only $2,500 (Figures 8.9 and 8.10).

Although Will-Spread can stand on its own, it can be used in conjunction with other known facts about the market. As just one example, you have read about a huge bias for stocks to rally at the first of every month, especially in February, March, May, July, September, October, and November. Thus one possible short-term strategy you could employ at the start of every month would be to take Will-Spread buy signals when the positive crossings occur, with special focus on the previously named months. Here is a recap of all such signals for 1997 starting with January. Stay with me as I "walk" and talk you through what happened and what you could realistically could have done using this combination of ingredients.

Figure 8.9   S&P 500 Index (30-minute bars). Graphed by the "Navigator" (Genesis Financial Data Services)

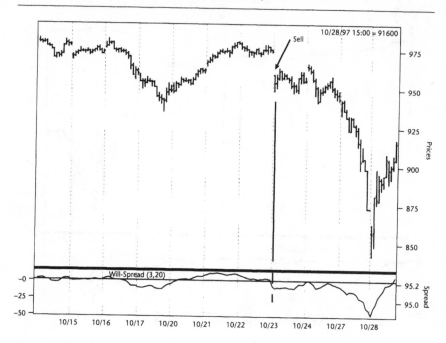

January 1997   Will-Spread did its thing crossing on January 2, 1997, with an entry at 744.70, staying positive until the negative crossing on January 6; by then the S&P rallied to 752.00 with a profit of 7.30 points!

February 1997   On January 29, the first-of-the-month rally was clearly indicated by a positive crossing at a price of 774.60 with an exit two days later on the close of January 31 as Will-Spread had begun to deteriorate. We know this is a 2- to 3-day bias, so let's take the 13.90 profit at the end of our time window unless the index is particularly bullish.

March 1997   We did not get an entry until March 3 at 792.90. This was not much of a trade, but took out 1.10 points profit with a crossing on March 4 when the S&P was trading at 794.00.

Figure 8.10 S&P 500 Index (30-minute bars). Graphed by the "Navigator" (Genesis Financial Data Services)

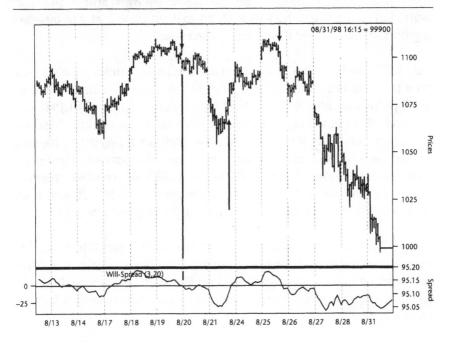

April 1997 Oh, I just love Will-Spread. A conventional month-end trader would have bought and lost money. But, you and I are smarter, we do not trade just technical and seasonal stuff alone, we know inner-market relationships provide meaningful insights into what is going on. That is why we bypassed the trade. Will-Spread did not give a buy until April 7, way outside the hot zone.

May 1997 We could see the month-end rally coming on April 28 when a bullish signal was given at 772.40 with an exit on May 1, 1997 at 800.50. This was a quick and explosive trade for an amazing 28.10 points profit!

June 1997 Here comes our first losing trade: a buy was given on May 28 with a positive crossing that went negative just a few bars later at 851.20. I would have pitched this trade the same day at

849.00 for a loss of 2.3 points. But, the hot zone of month-end/start was still there, so when Will-Spread turned positive on May 30, there was no reason not to take the trade; we were still in the time zone. Entry price was 844.70 with an exit on June 2 at 848.00 making up the loss on our first shot at the trade.

July 1997 Well, we are given another lesson in humility, going long on a positive crossing on June 30 at 896 with an exit the same day, a 6.0 point loss at 890! Wow, that was quick and ugly. But just like the end of June, we see another positive crossing on July 1, so we go long at 898. Our strategy is simple, wait for a negative crossing or two days in the trade. We wait. Will-Spread crosses to the downside just a few hours later at 897.80 for a .20 loss. Another crossing comes late in the day on July 1, so we reenter at 900.25 and hold until our sell on July 7 at 927.55, netting 21.10 points in July.

August 1997 Along comes the first of the month, but Will-Spread is tracking in the negative area so we have no trade. Again, our filter has kept us out of what appeared on the surface to be bullish. As the time approached, we could see the fundamentals were not there to justify the trade.

September 1997 More humility. There is a clear-cut crossing on August 29 with an equally clear-cut exit and loss the same day at 902.55 for our biggest loss of the year of 3.20 points.

But we stick with it, taking the buy signal on September 2 at 912.50 and watch a very powerful rally unfold lasting until September 3 when we close out the trade at 928.90, again recouping our earlier loss. That was close, but the combination of the time influence and inner market influence coupled to keep us in the black, with this 15.50 point gain +1295.

October 1997 We had to wait until the first of the month when a crossing took place forewarning us a rally was on the way. There was an additional chance to buy again as Will-Spread dipped into negative for one bar, but with no follow-through for a sell and an immediate upturn on October 2 at 965.30, giving another positive crossing until time ran out with a negative crossing. The rally stopped, for us at least, at 968.75, a 3.45 point gain.

November 1997 This was almost too easy. The crossing came on October 31 at 919.00 with an equally clear exit at 947 for a very profitable trade of 28.0 points. This is how I wish it worked every month!

December 1997 Another storybook trade with a positive crossing on the first of the month at 962.50 and an exit on December 2 at 973.20. It was, as old Blue Eyes used to sing, a "very good year," 13 total trades with 10 winners. More importantly, the net profits of 99.70 points, or $24,925, illustrate the validity of combining fundamentals with time influences. The time influence is always there, but without a valid underpinning—the stage being set on a fundamental basis—I will pass, thank you. There are too many good trading opportunities where we can get such high odds that there is no reason to go slumming for trades just because there is one element "that may work."

The more the merrier, that is my adage!

chapter 9

special short-term situations

It is time to develop a checklist of possible trading opportunities we can accept or reject each month. You can do this yourself by gleaning out of my work trading opportunities that appeal to you. To give you a feel for doing this, I devote this chapter to setting up specific trades you should be looking for each month. These trades are based on times of the month and holidays.

The time-of-the-month trade is hardly a new idea—the concept has been known for years. Here are my improvements and adaptations to a long-standing market truism: Stock prices rally around the first of the month. The light I shed on this play was to find out that Bond prices experience this same monthly uplift as demonstrated earlier. We will now develop a winning strategy based on these insights.

Month-End Trading in Stock Indexes

There are now several vehicles speculators can use to catch these swings. The S&P 500 stock index has been the kingpin of trading stock market moves, but lately, the lower margin S&P minicontract has been grabbing smaller investors' attention. The newcomer in this group, though, is the Dow Jones 30 index, a futures contract that mimics the world-famous Dow Jones Average. I expect this to become an even more important index to trade in the future.

Figure 9.1   S&P 500 buying first day of each month

```
Data            : S&P 500 IND-9967     09/80
Calc Dates      : 09/18/87 - 08/31/98

Num. Conv. P. Value  Comm  Slippage  Margin  Format  Drive:\Path\FileName
---------------------------------------------------------------------------
 149    2  $   2.500  $  0   $   0   $ 3,000  CT/PC  C:\GD\BACK67MS\F59.DAT

//////////////////////////////// ALL TRADES  - Test 3 \\\\\\\\\\\\\\\\\\\\\\\\\\\\\\\\

Total net profit          $73,437.50
Gross profit             $103,250.00   Gross loss               $-29,812.50

Total # of trades              129     Percent profitable               85%
Number winning trades          110     Number losing trades              19

Largest winning trade    $6,700.00     Largest losing trade      $-2,437.50
Average winning trade      $938.64     Average losing trade      $-1,569.08
Ratio avg win/avg loss        0.59     Avg trade (win & loss)       $569.28

Max consecutive winners         20     Max consecutive losers             2
Avg # bars in winners            1     Avg # bars in losers               1

Max closed-out drawdown  $-3,325.00    Max intra-day drawdown    $-3,950.00
Profit factor                 3.46     Max # of contracts held            1
Account size required    $6,950.00     Return on account              1,056%
```

The strategies discussed here are based on the S&P 500 for one simple reason; we have more data because this stock index began trading in 1982, the Dow 30 in 1997. But, the strategies can be applied to all the stock indexes; just alter your stop based on margin, contract size, and current volatility.

I went back to 1982 and tested buying the S&P 500 index on the open of the first trade day of every month with an exit on the first profitable opening. The stop I chose was only $1,500, but was not used on the day of entry; however, after the entry day it was in place at all times. There have been 129 trades making a net gain of $73,437, about $7,000 a year for trading only once a month. The numbers of this system are excellent; the accuracy is 85 percent, average profit per trade (that's net gain, winners minus losers, divided by total trades). Drawdown came in at $3,325, less than 5 percent of total gains. This is good stuff (see Figure 9.1).

Target Months

If you are getting the hang of this game, you may have already asked yourself if some months do better than others. The answer is

Table 9.1   Profitable S&P trades by month

Month	Net Profit	Number of Trades +/– Total
January	2,325	9/11
February	3,437	8/11
March	5,650	9/10
April	5,437	10/11
May	6,075	9/10
June	6,500	10/11
July	5,875	9/11
August	12,500	9/10
September	5,557	9/10
October	1,150	8/11
November	10,500	11/11
December	8,150	9/11

yes, as the following printouts show. The story they tell is that the worst months, in the past 16 years, have been January, February, and October. These should be your target months to avoid or be cautious of seasonal trading. I suggest you study the month-by-month recaps presented in Table 9.1.

Making It Better

Although some of our speculative competitors are aware of this repetitive pattern, most do not consistently take advantage of it nor have they figured out about skipping some months. That is a big improvement, but we can do even better.

How? By only taking these first-of-the-month trades when Bonds are in an uptrend. As I demonstrated earlier, an uptrend in Bonds is conducive to stock market rallies. A pretty good rule, and easy to follow, is to only buy on the first of a month—any month— if Bonds have closed higher the day prior to our anticipated entry than 30 days ago. This is evidence Bonds should be supportive of a stock market rally.

Month-End Trading in the Bond Market

Next, let's look at buying the first trading day of every month in the Bonds, as we did in the S&P 500. The results are quite profitable based on the rules of using an $1,100 stop and exiting on the first profitable opening. This approach to trading comes close to 70 percent accuracy and has a very large average profit per trade considering that we are in for only one day on average (see Figure 9.2).

We can dramatically improve these results if we simply bypassing the poorer performing months which, as shown in Table 9.2, are January, February, April, and October, with December being a question mark.

As mentioned, the month-end up move in stocks has been written about for years; all I have done is figure out how to better qualify trades for this time period. Until now, the tendency for Bonds to rally at this same time has been known by only a few of my students. My research and actual trading over the years show this is also an excellent time for short-term swing moves in Bonds and Bills.

Figures 9.3 and 9.4 should give you an overall view of this technique's strength. Figure 9.3 shows the growth in an account that would have bought one contract of T-Bonds on the third to the last

---

Figure 9.2   Bonds buying first day of each month

```
Data           : DAY T-BONDS-9967    01/80
Calc Dates     : 01/01/86 - 08/28/98

Num. Conv. P. Value  Comm  Slippage  Margin  Format  Drive:\Path\FileName
-----------------------------------------------------------------------------
  44   -5  $  31.250  $  0   $  0    $ 3,000  CT/PC   C:\GD\BACK67MS\F62.DAT

//////////////////////////////// ALL TRADES  - Test 1 \\\\\\\\\\\\\\\\\\\\\\\\\\\\\
Total net profit        $32,593.75
Gross profit            $83,531.25     Gross loss              $-50,937.50

Total # of trades            149       Percent profitable             69%
Number winning trades        104       Number losing trades            45

Largest winning trade   $2,593.75      Largest losing trade     $-1,375.00
Average winning trade     $803.19      Average losing trade     $-1,131.94
Ratio avg win/avg loss      0.70       Avg trade (win & loss)      $218.75

Max consecutive winners        8       Max consecutive losers           6
Avg # bars in winners          2       Avg # bars in losers             1

Max closed-out drawdown $-6,812.50     Max intra-day drawdown   $-7,437.50
Profit factor               1.63       Max # of contracts held          1
Account size required   $10,437.50     Return on account             312%
```

Table 9.2   Profits in bonds by month

Month	Net Profit	Number of Trades +/- Total
January	-31	8/13
February	-1,718	7/13
March	2,781	9/12
April	-343	8/13
May	6,125	9/12
June	3,125	13/9
July	1,093	8/13
August	4,343	9/12
September	7,187	11/12
October	-218	12/7
November	8,150	12/12
December	1,500	7/12

Figure 9.3   End-of-month T-bonds system (U.S. T-bonds day session 1983–1996)

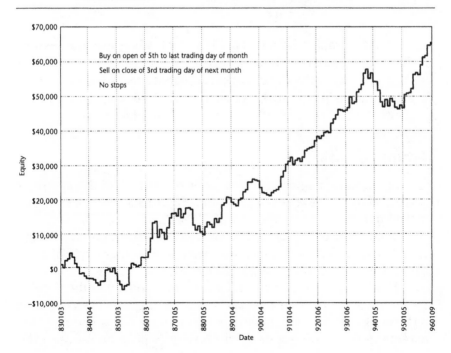

Figure 9.4   End-of-month S&P 500 (1983–1996)

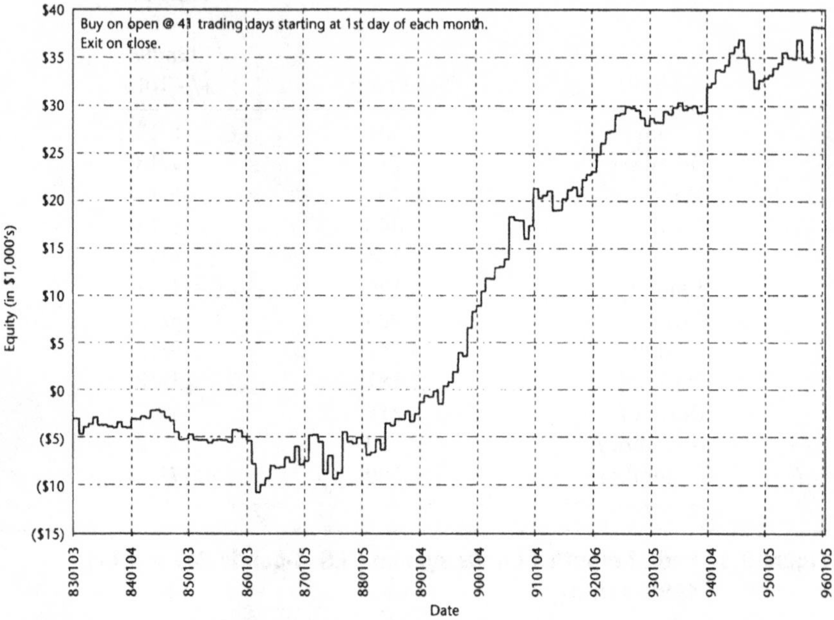

trading day of each month and held for six trading sessions, exiting at that time or taking a loss of $1,500 with a protective stop. This chart, from one of the Bond market's best students Mike Stock, offers convincing proof of the phenomenon. The same opportunity presents itself in the S&P 500 as well as Figure 9.4 shows.

Getting Specific

The rally usually begins in Bonds prior to the first of the month as evidenced by the next set of printouts. Figure 9.5 shows the results of buying Bonds on the opening of TDM 18 with a $1,500 stop and exiting on the close 3 days after entry. The 139 trades since 1986 netted $34,875 with a comfortable average profit per trade of $250. This is tradable, despite the $8,625 drawdown.

We can do better, however, by bringing a subset of the trend of the Gold market to filter out bad or marginal trades. As described in the works of such major contributors to our understanding of the markets as Marty Zweig or John Murphy (whose books are must

Figure 9.5   Buying bonds on TDM 18

```
Data          : DAY T-BONDS-9967    01/80
Calc Dates    : 01/01/86 - 08/28/98

Num. Conv. P. Value  Comm  Slippage  Margin  Format  Drive:\Path\FileName
-----------------------------------------------------------------------------
  44   -5 $ 31.250  $  0   $   0   $ 3,000  CT/PC  C:\GD\BACK67MS\F62.DAT

////////////////////////////// ALL TRADES  - Test 3 \\\\\\\\\\\\\\\\\\\\\\\\\\\\\\
```

Total net profit	$34,875.00		
Gross profit	$95,843.75	Gross loss	$-60,968.75
Total # of trades	139	Percent profitable	71%
Number winning trades	99	Number losing trades	40
Largest winning trade	$2,812.50	Largest losing trade	$-1,906.25
Average winning trade	$968.12	Average losing trade	$-1,524.22
Ratio avg win/avg loss	0.63	Avg trade (win & loss)	$250.90
Max consecutive winners	17	Max consecutive losers	4
Avg # bars in winners	3	Avg # bars in losers	3
Max closed-out drawdown	$-8,625.00	Max intra-day drawdown	$-8,656.25
Profit factor	1.57	Max # of contracts held	1
Account size required	$11,656.25	Return on account	299%

reading), Gold exerts a great impact on Bonds. When Gold is in an uptrend, it acts as an impediment to Bond market rallies, conversely, when Gold is in a downtrend, Bonds are more apt to rally.

Figure 9.6 reveals the power of filtering trades with Gold. In this case, trades were taken at the same time period with the same

Figure 9.6   Bond TDM 18 buy signals backed by gold

```
Data          : DAY T-BONDS-9967    01/80
Calc Dates    : 01/01/86 - 08/28/98

Num. Conv. P. Value  Comm  Slippage  Margin  Format  Drive:\Path\FileName
-----------------------------------------------------------------------------
  44   -5 $ 31.250  $  0   $   0   $ 3,000  CT/PC  C:\GD\BACK67MS\F62.DAT

////////////////////////////// ALL TRADES  - Test 3 \\\\\\\\\\\\\\\\\\\\\\\\\\\\\\
```

Total net profit	$32,062.50		
Gross profit	$65,093.75	Gross loss	$-33,031.25
Total # of trades	90	Percent profitable	75%
Number winning trades	68	Number losing trades	22
Largest winning trade	$2,812.50	Largest losing trade	$-1,531.25
Average winning trade	$957.26	Average losing trade	$-1,501.42
Ratio avg win/avg loss	0.63	Avg trade (win & loss)	$356.25
Max consecutive winners	11	Max consecutive losers	3
Avg # bars in winners	3	Avg # bars in losers	3
Max closed-out drawdown	$-4,500.00	Max intra-day drawdown	$-4,500.00
Profit factor	1.97	Max # of contracts held	1
Account size required	$7,500.00	Return on account	427%

stop and exit as before. The difference is that trades were only taken if Gold was in a downtrend (i.e., the close of Gold on the day prior to entry was less than 24 days ago). Although total profits dip $2,000, the accuracy slightly increases while our all important average profit per trade jumps over $100 per trade and drawdown improves substantially by being cut almost in half!

Better and Better

We can do even better than the preceding results by delaying our entry until TDM 22. There are a lot less trades as the Figure 9.7 shows, only 50, but a higher accuracy, 76 percent, an amazing $496 average profit per trade, and very livable drawdown of a little over $4,500.

I know, I know, you want to know what happens when we back this trading opportunity with the trend of Gold. Well, Figure 9.8 shows the answers and they are very impressive, $20,156 of profits. Again, the trend criteria is that Gold close lower than 24 days ago, same stop and exit as in the previous results. Although our drawdown has a major improvement, crashing all the way down to $1,500, the accuracy skyrockets to 89 percent and average profit literally zooms to $719 per trade.

Figure 9.7   Bond TDM 22 buy signals

```
Data           : DAY T-BONDS-9967    01/80
Calc Dates     : 01/01/86 - 08/28/98

Num. Conv. P. Value  Comm  Slippage  Margin  Format  Drive:\Path\FileName
-----------------------------------------------------------------------------
  44  -5  $  31.250  $  0  $  0   $  3,000  CT/PC   C:\GD\BACK67MS\F62.DAT

//////////////////////////// ALL TRADES  - Test 3 \\\\\\\\\\\\\\\\\\\\\\\\\\\\
Total net profit        $24,812.50
Gross profit            $42,812.50    Gross loss              $-18,000.00

Total # of trades             50    Percent profitable             76%
Number winning trades         38    Number losing trades           12

Largest winning trade   $2,718.75    Largest losing trade    $-1,500.00
Average winning trade   $1,126.64    Average losing trade    $-1,500.00
Ratio avg win/avg loss        0.75    Avg trade (win & loss)     $496.25

Max consecutive winners        7    Max consecutive losers          3
Avg # bars in winners          3    Avg # bars in losers            2

Max closed-out drawdown $-4,500.00    Max intra-day drawdown  $-4,593.75
Profit factor                2.37    Max # of contracts held         1
Account size required   $7,593.75    Return on account             326%
```

Figure 9.8   Bond TDM 22 buy signals backed by gold

```
Data          : DAY T-BONDS-9967    01/80
Calc Dates    : 01/01/86 - 08/28/98

Num. Conv. P. Value  Comm  Slippage  Margin  Format  Drive:\Path\FileName
-------------------------------------------------------------------------
  44   -5  $ 31.250  $ 0   $  0    $ 3,000  CT/PC   C:\GD\BACK67MS\F62.DAT

////////////////////////////// ALL TRADES  - Test 2 \\\\\\\\\\\\\\\\\\\\\\\\\\\\\\

Total net profit          $20,156.25
Gross profit              $24,656.25    Gross loss                $-4,500.00

Total # of trades                 28    Percent profitable               89%
Number winning trades             25    Number losing trades              3

Largest winning trade      $2,468.75    Largest losing trade      $-1,500.00
Average winning trade        $986.25    Average losing trade      $-1,500.00
Ratio avg win/avg loss          0.65    Avg trade (win & loss)       $719.87

Max consecutive winners           17    Max consecutive losers            1
Avg # bars in winners              2    Avg # bars in losers              1

Max closed-out drawdown   $-1,500.00    Max intra-day drawdown    $-2,093.75
Profit factor                   5.47    Max # of contracts held           1
Account size required      $5,093.75    Return on account               395%
```

This is an exceptional trading opportunity; the problem is not many months have a TDM 22, but when they do, I will be buying. Check out the string of winners with the Gold filter, 17 winners in a row, whereas without the filter, we only had 5 winners in a row.

A Time to Sell as Well

Bonds have also dipped around mid-month most of the time, as Figure 9.9 reveals. The rules called for selling on the open of TDM 12 with our usual 3-day exit and $1,400 stop. From 1986 to the middle of 1998, this dip has been profitable to trade 76 percent of the time with an average profit per trade of $133 on the 152 trades. Drawdown is acceptable at $6,093, but larger than the ideal ratio of profits to drawdown. Ideally, drawdown should be no more than 15 percent of the profits of $20,281. In this case, the drawdown was 20 percent profits. So, although we are certainly onto something here, I would like a shot at making it better.

Whereas traditional commodity market analysts would try to filter this trading opportunity with technical "junk" like the trend, oscillators, or momentum flows, I would rather go back to what matters; fundamental relationships, that of Gold to Bonds. After

Figure 9.9   Bond sells TDM 12

```
Data          : DAY T-BONDS-9967    01/80
Calc Dates    : 01/01/86 - 08/28/98
```

```
Num. Conv. P. Value  Comm  Slippage  Margin  Format  Drive:\Path\FileName
------------------------------------------------------------------------
  44   -5  $ 31.250  $ 0   $  0   $ 3,000  CT/PC   C:\GD\BACK67MS\F62.DAT
```

//////////////////////////// ALL TRADES - Test 3 \\\\\\\\\\\\\\\\\\\\\\\\\\\\

Total net profit	$20,281.25		
Gross profit	$73,375.00	Gross loss	$-53,093.75
Total # of trades	152	Percent profitable	76%
Number winning trades	117	Number losing trades	35
Largest winning trade	$3,000.00	Largest losing trade	$-2,000.00
Average winning trade	$627.14	Average losing trade	$-1,516.96
Ratio avg win/avg loss	0.41	Avg trade (win & loss)	$133.43
Max consecutive winners	13	Max consecutive losers	3
Avg # bars in winners	2	Avg # bars in losers	3
Max closed-out drawdown	$-6,093.75	Max intra-day drawdown	$-6,250.00
Profit factor	1.38	Max # of contracts held	1
Account size required	$9,250.00	Return on account	219%

all, charts and oscillators do not move the market, underlying conditions do.

In addition to now having a real way to trade this mid-month dip, we are also able to again see the power of fundamentals in Figure 9.10. The trade entry and exit rules are exactly as in the previous

Figure 9.10   Bond sells TDM backed by gold

```
Data          : DAY T-BONDS-9967    01/80
Calc Dates    : 01/01/86 - 08/28/98
```

```
Num. Conv. P. Value  Comm  Slippage  Margin  Format  Drive:\Path\FileName
------------------------------------------------------------------------
  44   -5  $ 31.250  $ 0   $  0   $ 3,000  CT/PC   C:\GD\BACK67MS\F62.DAT
```

//////////////////////////// ALL TRADES - Test 4 \\\\\\\\\\\\\\\\\\\\\\\\\\\\

Total net profit	$26,250.00		
Gross profit	$50,250.00	Gross loss	$-24,000.00
Total # of trades	73	Percent profitable	78%
Number winning trades	57	Number losing trades	16
Largest winning trade	$2,656.25	Largest losing trade	$-1,500.00
Average winning trade	$881.58	Average losing trade	$-1,500.00
Ratio avg win/avg loss	0.58	Avg trade (win & loss)	$359.59
Max consecutive winners	14	Max consecutive losers	3
Avg # bars in winners	3	Avg # bars in losers	3
Max closed-out drawdown	$-4,500.00	Max intra-day drawdown	$-4,593.75
Profit factor	2.09	Max # of contracts held	1
Account size required	$7,593.75	Return on account	345%

clip, the only difference—and what a difference it makes—is that trades were only taken when Gold had closed greater than the close 10 days ago. In other words, Gold was in an uptrend, which suggests to us that sell signals should be more effective in this monetary environment. The average profit per trade more than doubles, profits get bumped up $6,000, accuracy goes from 76 percent to 78 percent, no big deal, but our drawdown to profit percentage is just about halved from 20.9 percent to 11 percent. Perhaps best of all the average profit per trade jumps to $359 from $133.

Here we have a very tradable opportunity. All one need do is have the patience to wait for the mid-month time periods when Gold has been in an uptrend: That is the fundamental setup that created these results.

Patience seems to be the one commodity in short supply among commodity traders. I want to wager or speculate only when I have a distinct advantage in the game.

chapter 10

when to get out
of your trades

I have three rules for you to follow to get out of your short-term trades:

1. Always use a dollar stop on all trades so in the event all else fails, you will have protection.

2. Use my "bailout" profit-taking technique developed with the help of Ralph Vince. The basic rule is to exit on the first profitable opening. If the profit is only one tick, take it.

   This works best for the S&P; for slower moving markets, I will delay the bailout a day or two to give the market time to grow thus increasing my average profit per trade.

3. Exit and reverse if you get an opposite signal. If you are short and get a buy signal, don't wait for the stop or bailout exit, go with the most current signal.

That is all I have to tell you about exits. Don't get greedy, let the rules, not your emotions, take care of your trades.

part three

strategy and summary

chapter 11

thoughts on the business of speculation

It is one thing to correctly call the twists and turns of the markets, but that is not how long-term wealth is created, nor is that talent sufficient, in and of itself, for a career in this business.

Career success does not mean you have ferreted out a winning trade or two. Anyone can do that at any given time. That is not a career that is either getting lucky or getting good. The business end of speculation amounts to consistently doing the right thing—not getting off track, down in the dumps over the current losing trade or floating in the sky because you have had two winners in a row. I am much more interested in the career aspect of this art than I am in the last trade or two. Anyone can drive a nail or two into a board, but that is not what builds a house. To build a house, you need not only the skills, but also a plan, the intentions to follow and complete the plan, and the ability to show up every day, rain or shine.

What Speculation Is All About

The art of speculation is about figuring out the most probable direction the future will take. The future is seldom predictable to any precise level or event, yet all such investment predictions will entail three elements: *selection, timing,* and *management* of the prediction. Mastering one of these aspects is not adequate; you must understand and be proficient in all three of them, so let's take a look at each element.

There are two aspects of selection: one is selecting a market ready to move; the other is selecting so you can focus. Just because a market trades, don't expect your favorite commodity to suddenly have a rip-roaring move that will enrich your bank account. A study of any charted history of any stock or commodity will divulge an amazing secret that separates the would-be speculators from folks like you and me; price usually moves sideways in meandering back-and-forth pattern, perhaps with a slight trend direction. There are only three or four optimum times a year to take advantage of im-mediate and substantial changes in price. Go ahead, check some charts, see and learn for yourself that big price changes do not occur every day. In fact, they are less likely, rather than more likely, to take place . . . they are the exception, not the rule.

That is why trade selection is so important. You don't want to get stuck in the mud of a choppy, trendless market; it will wear you out or shake you out. In either event, you lose. If not money, time. It is imperative then, that you learn to know when a market has been set up and is ready to roar.

I have given you numerous setup considerations in this book that include TDM, TDW, holidays, and intermarket correlations. There are others, such as the net long or short positions of the largest (and therefore smartest) traders, the invariably wrong posi-tions of the public, even major news events that alter market activ-ity. A successful speculator plays a waiting game. Most people cannot wait, they would rather wager. The sooner the better. Spec-ulator kings and queens have the patience to put off taking action until the tumblers have clicked into place, knowing profits are then more likely to prevail.

There is another reason selection can be paramount to profits. I have always done the best when I have traded just one or two mar-kets. By eliminating all the others, the distractions, I have been able to thoroughly learn how my selected markets operate, what moves them, and perhaps of even greater importance, what does not move them. No great accomplishment has ever come about without fo-cusing talent, intentions, and action. This business is no different. The more focused you are on what you are doing, the more suc-cessful you will become.

This thought fits well with the way business works. Heart spe-cialists make more money than general practitioners. In this day and age of complexity, specialization has a large payoff. Years ago, I heard about a wise trader who made millions in the stock market. He lived high in the Sierra Mountains and would call his broker about three times a year always to buy or sell the same stock. His broker told me the man had indeed amassed a fortune, all from this one stock, by using financial focus.

It's about Time

If you are now focused on a specific commodity that your new tools and techniques, and dreams say you should soon have a tradable move, it is still not time to rush in. Selection is about what should move; timing, the next element of speculation, is about precisely when that should happen. Timing is about narrowing down when price change should begin. Tools you can use here are simple trend-lines, volatility breakouts, patterns, and the like. The essence of timing is to let the market prove to you that it is ready to explode in your selected direction.

Just what does that mean? In case of wanting to go long, I can tell you this; a decline in price sure as heck does not mean the up-side explosion has begun. *Au contraire!* A price decline suggests further price decline: It is that simple Newtonian idea that an object once set in motion continues to stay in motion. Traders have a great conflict going at all times, we want to buy, thus conventional logic says to buy at the cheapest possible price. Yet trend analysis says don't buy what is going down! My advice is to forget buying cheap. Buy when the explosion has begun. Yes, you will miss catching the low, but that is far better than having new lows in price catch you!

Trade Management

The third aspect of speculation deals with how you manage the trade itself as well as the money you are committing to the trade. Traditional wisdom is that you should not trade with money you cannot afford to lose.

Maybe.

But consider this, if your mind-set is that this is play money, I assure you that you will play with it. And probably lose. If it is real money—money *you cannot afford to lose*—the chances that you will pay close attention are much greater, and so are your chances of winning. Necessity is not only the mother of invention but also the control of speculation.

Trade management goes beyond money management as it relates to how long you will stay in the trade and how much profit to take. It directly concerns itself with your emotions: this means not getting carried away; it means not overtrading, not undertrading; it means doing the right thing and managing your emotional state during the trade.

Knowing how to trade is not the same as knowing how to win at trading. The art of trading combines selection and entry techniques with money management. That is the essence of what needs to be done, but the superior trader understands that it is the management—the control or the use of these techniques—that maximizes market profits.

Essential Points about Speculation

Rich People Don't Make Big Bets

Rich people, who are generally smart, have learned that you don't bet the farm on one spin of the wheel, investment deal, or trade. Wannabe speculators are consumed with the notion that they will amass tons of money very quickly by making a killing. They become the hapless victims, as in the process they have become plungers. Yes, you can plunge once or twice in your life, but if you consistently plunge, you will lose on one of these wagers, and since you are betting it all, you will lose it all. That is why rich people don't make big bets.

They are far too shrewd to risk all they have on an investment, as they know investment decisions can be random. In their wisdom, they know the future is somewhat unpredictable; hence they play the game that way. Years ago, I was on the board of directors of a small bank in Montana and in that position reviewed many loan requests. The business applications always included a pro forma, a projection of how the business would do, and how the loan could be repaid.

I don't think I ever saw any pro forma of what should happen become a reality! They were always off target, and as you might imagine, the reality of the business was not as prosperous as the pro forma would have led one to believe. An old-time banker had a great saying, "Nothing good ever comes in certified mail and pro formas are never right."

Rich people make more money by finding a good investment or two, and investing an optimal amount in those investments. There is no need to take the risk of being wiped out in exchange for the thrill of plunging; it simply is not worth it.

To Make a Thousand, You've Got to Bet a Thousand

This is a favorite expression of pit bosses in Las Vegas and is a subset to the idea that rich people don't bet big:

> That's the favorite expression of Las Vegas pit bosses, and it's dead wrong. Here's the right way to "make a thousand."

There is not that much difference between gambling and speculation. The big compelling contrast is that gamblers can never get a leg up on the game, the odds are against them all the time (unless they count cards and play blackjack). It has always amazed me that in a game where the odds are against us, we flock to the table to play.

Las Vegas stays open 24 hours a day for a simple reason; players won't quit and in any endeavor where you have an advantage, especially a slight one, the longer you play the more certain you are of winning. So they never stop. To casinos, the public is the bank account they tap every minute of every day.

Weaknesses of the Pit Boss Adage   Pit bosses are supposed gurus of gambling knowledge; after all, they have seen it all. But the advice that to make a thousand you need to bet a thousand is "house talk" that will get you into serious trouble.

Last year, my daughter traded $10,000 to $110,000, while I took an account from $50,000 to over $1,000,000. At no time did we make "a big bet." It was quite the contrary, our bet size was small, never risking more than 20 percent of our stake and *that was larger than it should have been or needed to be.*

If you have an advantage in the game, as a speculator must before deciding to play, then play by the real rule that has kept Las Vegas building all those extravagant Meccas of money: risk little and play around the clock.

The problem with betting a thousand to make a thousand is you can lose that thousand just as quickly. So why not seek out a strategy that makes a thousand by the natural growth of the game, not by the luck or lack of it on the next trade. There is plenty of money to be made trading and the game is not going to get shut down anytime soon, so learn to harvest your winnings over time, not on one roll of the dice.

In my 36 years of following the markets, I have seen more people lose fortunes than make them. The losers—all of them—did the opposite of the winners, they bet big thinking they could make a killing on one or two trades. The winners made their fortunes by consistently doing the right thing. When you step out to make a killing, you are more likely to be killed than to survive.

Why Rich People Don't Make Big Bets Really rich—and smart—people don't make big bets. First they are not out to "prove" anything, they are out to make more money, and second, they know that risk control is as important as the other two legs of speculation, selection and timing. *That is all this business of commodity trading gets down to—selection, timing, and risk control.*

Speculation Is for People Who Love Roller Coasters
Trust me on this. If you don't like the thrill and up-and-down gyrations of a roller coaster, put this book down, ask for your money back and go on with your humdrum life. The life of a speculator is literally one roller coaster ride after another; it is a series of ups and downs, highs and lows where hopefully the lows are progressively higher, but the reality is often the lows are lower. Worse yet, so are the highs!

Although many are attracted to the life of speculation because of the thrill, they don't envision the ups and downs, they think it will be a steady stream of Rolls Royce limousines and lollipops. It is not; it's a steady stream of unknown, free-form verse that at times seemingly leads nowhere. In this business, thrill kills.

You must, at heart, be a thrill seeker. But you cannot let that take over your trading style; indeed, if you do not learn to corral or harness your thrill-seeking nature, you will never make it as a speculator. That is probably what makes this business so difficult; while it takes a thrill seeker to speculate, it takes a risk-aversive person to make a career out of speculation. What you must have to succeed in this business, you also must learn to regulate, to control. Clamp down on the roller coaster or it will jump the track. My advice to be a long-term winner in the game of speculation is this: kill thrill.

If You Don't Have the Patience to Wait, There Will Be Nothing to Wait For

This is one of the elements of thrill you must learn to control. Thrill seekers, like you and me (I include you because you didn't put this book down and are still reading), enjoy the rush we get from the experience so much that we want it all the time; hence the neophyte speculator will trade, wager, at the drop of a hat. Set up a proposition and he or she will plunk down money, simply because win or lose, there's a sure payoff—the rush.

The core problem new commodity traders have is what we call "overtrading." This comes about when traders look more for an adrenaline high than for market profits. They find this by either (a) trading more often than they should or (b) trading more contracts than they should.

It is really a question of intensity: The more contracts you have, the more thrill you will experience. The more often you trade, the more often you will get an injection of endorphins pumping through your brain. These, then, are *your mortal enemies:* too many trades or too many contracts. Rich people don't bet big and they don't bet hyperactively.

Patience dictates that you trade for a reason beyond the rush, beyond the swashbuckling images we carry in our minds of what a speculator does and thinks. Frequency and intensity, in my world of speculation, are not bigger and better. I want to be selective, to wait for the ideal time to take my very best shot. This is certainly not a business of scattergun shooting; we are like hunters waiting in the bushes until our game is in full view and about three feet away. Then and only then should we fire away!

Impatient traders literally use up all their ammunition, money, and emotions, so when it is time to shoot, their guns are empty.

If You Can't Follow It, What Good Is a System or Strategy?

Technicians and the like are forever developing trading systems to beat the pants off the market. They spend thousands of hours and dollars in pursuit of profits. That is good; I do the same thing almost every day of my life in an attempt to seek greater understanding of the markets.

The difference is once they have arrived at their "master system" they take a trade or two and then begin either tinkering with the system or overruling what it is telling them to do. Years ago, my longtime friend Lin Eldridge put it best, "Why keep a system and do all that work if you're not going to follow it?"

Be honest with yourself. If you are not going to abide by the rules you create, why create the rules? You should be spending your time doing something else. When it comes to speculation, rules are not made to be broken unless you want to end up broke. The rules of speculation exist to tell the ideal time to get in and out, but more importantly the rules exist to protect us from ourselves.

Maybe you think this is not your problem, that following a system is an easy thing to do. It isn't.

Last year in America almost 52,000 people were killed—about 1,000 a week—in car accidents because they failed to obey one of two very simple rules, don't speed and/or don't drive if you have been drinking. Those are easy rules, not complex, not chock-full of emotions like the rules of speculation. Yet families went through major turmoil and grief due to those unexpected wrecks caused by not following a very simple system. Should you choose to speculate in a swashbuckling fashion, trust me, the financial results will be the same. There most assuredly will be carnage and ruin on your speculative highways.

The law of gravity always prevails and the law of gravity in our business must be obeyed.

Christmas Doesn't Come in December

Here is the real rub with this business of being a commodity trader or speculator; we never, ever, know when we will make our money for the year.

Owners of jewelry stores know they will make most of their money around the holidays or at Christmas. That is true of most retail stores; they know when the money is going to roll in and can plan for that event.

We cannot. That's one reason I have written books and published a newsletter; I wanted a sense of some steady income in my life, plus it is profitable! I may make money hand over fist for 12 months running or make nothing, in fact lose money, for the first 6 or 7 months of the year then hit the jackpot. One never knows in this world of roller coasters what will happen.

That is why commodity fund managers take a flat percentage of the assets under management. That way, they have steady income to offset their costs, despite the typical 20 percent of the profits they charge. They, like anyone else, need to have a consistent income stream.

To my way of thinking, most of you should not quit your jobs and become traders. Your job, as bad as it might be, is your security, your source of income, the guaranteed Christmas. Yes, I know you don't like your job, but you know what? I don't like mine every day either. It is no piece of cake getting beat up in the markets for 2 to 3 months. It is no joy to have a series of bad market calls in a newsletter where everyone can see the errors of my way—errors my enemies love to magnify and my best friends chuckle over.

But, none of that matters. In my world, I know you don't have to like it, you just have to do it. That means I must continue following a system, even while it is in a drawdown losing money, I must use stops when I don't feel like it, and I must keep telling myself Christmas may be delayed this year. What is more, I had better budget and plan my personal life accordingly; I must have enough cash to get me through an extended Christmas drought. And finally, if I do get lucky and find Christmas comes this year in January or February, I sure as heck can't expect it will be Christmas every day until December 25. There are no straight paths to heaven, my account equity is not a straight-up line, it is a meandering backroad that encounters plenty of peaks and valleys. That is why I never know when Christmas will come. I just know if I do the right things, eventually Santa will find my chimney.

If You Have an Advantage in the Game, the Longer You Play the Greater Your Chances Are of Winning

If you know you have an advantage in the game, you know that at some point you will be collecting the chips, that Christmas will come.

This is a vital concept for all speculators, it is a concept to build a belief system on, but the concept itself cannot be built on a belief. Casinos don't operate on a belief. They operate, run their business, on pure math; they know that eventually the laws of the wheel or dice will prevail. Thus they keep the wheels spinning. They don't mind waiting, they don't stop. They also play 24 hours for a reason; the longer you play their negative expectation game, the more certain they are of getting your money.

I guess that is why I have always been amused by people who think they can go to Las Vegas to tap the casino's bank. Casinos look at you and me as fodder for their bank accounts, and judging from the size of the megahotels as well as stock performance, they are on the right side of the ledger.

As traders, we must realize that time is our ally. Legal contracts say time is of the essence; that may be so when it comes to performance of obligations, but time is not of the essence when it comes to trading because, given an advantage in a game, the more time that elapses the more certain your eventual winnings.

Casinos don't close for another reason; the players won't quit. Players overtrade, in our vernacular.

We are not casinos but we can sure learn a great deal from them. We need to know for sure that our approach has a statistical advantage in the game. You need to test, to prove your strategy. You cannot just assume what you are doing will make money because you are so darn smart or good looking. Once you have proven through research that your approach works, it is then just a question of backing your convictions by following the system.

Press Your Winners, Not Your Losers

This is the most important underlying rule of speculation. Losers do the opposite: They increase the size of their bets when losing and decrease their bets when winning! Losers see a guy lose all his money at a slot machine and rush in to take his place!

Winners look for positive streaks and press their advantage. I vividly recall a string of 18 winning trades in a row in the S&P 500 on a hot line I used to do. After 3 winning trades in a row, 75 percent of the subscribers would not take the next trades; after 6 winners in a row, no one took any more trades!

What is going on here is that the human mind cannot stand success and seemingly loves failure. People fear that winnings will turn into failure, whereas they apparently have more hope that failure will turn into success, so they willingly invest or speculate following losses.

The truth is, success is the result of strings of winning trades, and to succeed you must not stop because you have been successful. Press the winnings. Failure is the result of strings of losing trades; the most certain indication that a system is failing is that it is experiencing strings of losses greater than seen in the past, exactly what the typical speculator is seeking to take advantage of! Admittedly, there is wisdom in waiting for short-term failure to start investing in a long-term successful system, but there is no wisdom at all in stopping because something has been "too successful"!

Press your winnings, gang, not your losses.

Success Kills—Affluence Is Dangerous

Although we must, and will, press our winnings, we cannot let success go to our heads because affluence leads to overconfidence, which in turn leads to not following the rules that led to our success.

I have heard countless stories from traders who started following my approach and did very well, in some cases making over $100,000, then gave it all back. When pressed on what happened, the bottom line is always the same, the speculator confused luck and consistent application of valid rules with ego and ego prevailed.

Their ego told them they had finally arrived, they had enough money to take chances and didn't need the basics anymore. They were in charge! Thus they got into a "damn the torpedoes—full steam ahead" mode. No longer were stops so important, and since they were now trading too many positions or too many markets, when the hits came they were big. Too big—it was wipeout time.

How is this cured? There is a simple concept that I keep telling myself: You dance with the person you brought to the dance. Don't change because you see some other beautiful system or trading approach. If you are making money, stay with it, same rules, same logic—don't tinker. It has never been me that has made the money trading, it has been my following of some well-tested and proven systems or methodology. On my own, on your own, flying by the seat of your pants, you are headed for a crack-up. The more ego you involve and the further you stray from the operating rules of speculation, the sooner and the more spectacular the crash.

Confidence, Fear, and Aggressiveness

> The meek will never make it as speculators so they had better have an inheritance.

The three traits speculators must learn to manage within themselves are confidence, fear, and aggressiveness. I will discuss them in this order.

Confidence   You need to have some confidence but not too much. The confidence comes from your study of the market and not from your feelings about yourself. Forget that entire warm fuzzy inner-child good feeling about your self-confidence. What you need is confidence based on experience and research that allows you to take correct action without choking when it is time to place a trade. Losers choke. Winners feel nervous about the trade, but they have enough confidence in the approach they are using, not themselves, that they place the trade.

Without confidence, you will never be able to pull the trigger and take your trades, especially during tumultuous market times, which is usually when the best trades pop up out of nowhere.

The meek probably do inherit the earth because they sure as heck are not going to make any money on their own as speculators. The inner assurance I have seen in big-time commodity traders is inspirational. Its essence is not pluck or conceit, nor a sense of self-possession. What is at the core of their confidence is trust or faith that things will work out.

Winning traders see or believe in the future, to that extent they are full of faith. I believe in God, and that good prevails, that all things do work out favorably. If I don't let God down, I will not be let down. My belief that God prevails gives me the trust in the future to have enough confidence to trade when others fail to take action. I know my life will work out okay, that I have never doubted for an instant. Fear can be limiting, to the point a trader does not believe in the future.

We Have More to Fear than Fear Itself   Roosevelt had it all wrong about fear. That should come as no surprise, he single-handedly screwed up this great country more than any other leader ever has with his New Deal socialism and welfare state programs. Worse yet, he persuaded the masses and the media that his programs got us out of the Great Depression. Sure, like America would not have recovered or grown without him? I will never forget campaigning for the United States Senate in the general election and knocking on doors in a heavily Democratic district. Behind one of those doors was a wizened lady of at least 80 whose vote I asked for only to have her tell me she didn't vote. When I asked why, she said, "I voted only once in my life, that was for FDR, and after seeing what he did, I told myself that if I was dumb enough to vote for that son of a bitch, I should never vote again!"

Fear is a powerful force to help speculators perform at their peak. The best example of the use of fear that I know was expressed by Royce Gracie. You may not know who Royce Gracie is so let me tell you a bit about him.

Gracie is a world-class athlete, he is the guy in those Ultimate Fight pay-for-view TV shows. In case you haven't seen one, they are for-real fights, no boxing gloves and just about anything is legal from kicking to gouging. This is for real violence. What is interesting about Gracie is that in over 100 fights he has never been beaten. That is never as in never, ever. By anyone, boxers, kickers, elbow punchers, Tai kickers. No one has been able to beat this guy.

Considering that most of these would-be tough guys weigh from 225 to 300 pounds, Gracie's accomplished victories are even more awesome when you find out he weighs about 180 pounds and looks better in a Mr. Rogers sweater than fighting attire. You would never know the guy is a giant killer. Since I am fascinated with fighters and winners (they have a lot in common with speculators), I have followed this guy's career and listened intently to his words of wisdom.

In one interview, these television thugs were asked if they felt any fear going onto these fights because, after all, they are real— guys have been maimed, lost their sight, broken bones, suffered numerous severe concussions, and at least one fighter has died. All the tough guys machine-gunned out their male macho line about having no fear of anyone or anything.

That is all of them but Gracie. He freely admitted he is scared to death every time he enters the ring. He went on to say he uses that fear to his advantage as it enables him to respect his opponent and not take reckless action or deviate from his personal fighting style. "Without fear," he said, "you cannot win as fear pumps me up for the fight but also assures that I will not lose control. What we do is very dangerous; my best protection is to be afraid so I protect myself in all the ways of my craft."

Like Gracie, I have an immense fear of trading, I have seen people wiped out, losing all they owned from poor speculation. Some went bankrupt, some really did go crazy, and several killed themselves. I suspect all these people had one thing in common: They did not fear the markets.

I think you need to fear the markets and fear yourself.

Although the markets are frightening, the emotions you and I inject into trading are downright scary. Without fear, there is no respect; if you do not respect the markets and fear yourself, you will become one more dead body on the long trail of commodity market casualties scattered across the land.

The Right Dosage of Fear and Confidence Creates Aggressiveness
There comes a time in every trader's life, about once a week in fact, when you have to get aggressive, either in protecting yourself or asserting your market expectations. It is kind of like that eye of the Tiger thing in the old *Rocky* movie. Unless you have a killer instinct, you had better fold your tent and go home. This is not a business for passive people who seemingly don't care whether they win or lose, people who lack that cutting edge to pick up a challenge and proceed.

I don't mean hostility as most people usually envision aggressiveness. Winning traders have a certain boldness to their action, and that boldness is the culmination of confidence, fear, and aggressiveness. In this battle for speculative profits, a well-thought-out plan with boldness will go a long way toward carrying the day.

chapter 12

money management—the keys to the kingdom

Here it is, the most important chapter in this book, the most important chapter in my life, the most valuable thoughts I can transfer from me to you. I have nothing of more value that I could possibly give you than what you are about to learn. This is not an overstatement.

What I am going to explain is the formula I have used to take small amounts of money like $2,000 to over $40,000, $10,000 to $110,000, and $10,000 to $1,100,000. These were not hypothetical victories; we are not talking Monday morning quarterbacking—we are talking real time, real money, real profits that you can spend to buy all the luxuries of life.

Until you use a money management approach, you will be a two-bit speculator, making some money here, losing some there, but never making a big score. The brass ring of commodity trading will always be out of your grasp as you sashay from one trade to another, picking up dollars but not amassing wealth.

The truly shocking thing about money management is how few people want to hear about it or learn the correct formulas. When I am at a dinner or cocktail party, invariably the conversation turns to the markets. People want hot tips, or to know how I have been able to make a living without working. They want my secret. As if there is one!

The public or noneducated speculator thinks there is magic to trading, that somewhere, someplace, someone has a magic decoder ring that correctly signals market action.

Nothing could be further from the truth. Money is made in this business by getting an advantage in the game, working that advantage on a consistent basis, and coupling this with a consistent approach to how much of your bankroll you have behind each trade.

Most Traders Use a Hit-and-Miss Approach

Most traders who are confident enough to risk large sums of money are also confident enough to think they can figure out the future. That translates into two problem areas.

First, we think we can select the winning trades from the losers in our system or approach. Worst, though, is knowing we are smart enough to do that, we then trade an unequal number of contracts or shares on our various trades.

Just as we must consistently follow our battle plan to succeed, we must also be consistent in the amount of money we marshal behind each trade. The instant you get the notion you can "for sure" spot the big winners and back those trades with more contracts than you have been trading, trouble will find you.

Every now and then, you will hit it right and score big, but eventually, you will have a loss on that large position. The loss is bad enough, but since you have overstepped good money management, you will then become emotional and probably hold onto the trade too long in hopes of recouping the big hit. Thus things don't get better, they get worse!

Let me turn to our well-worn Las Vegas casino analogy one more time. Casinos all over the world limit their losses by having a maximum amount the player can bet on any one decision in every game. A good commodity trader should limit losses in the same way. Can you imagine a pit boss suddenly allowing a high roller to bet more than the house limit because the boss "feels" the customer is going to lose on the next roll? Of course not; the pit boss would be fired on the spot for breaking a cardinal rule of money management, risking too much.

Trading too much, betting too much will cost you far more than bad market calls.

Approaches to Money Management—One Is Right for You

There are many ways to go about this problem, many formulas to follow. But all the superior systems to manage your investment dollars have a common tenet; you will increase the number of units, contracts, or shares as you make money and decrease as you lose money. That is the essence of the sweet science of the correct marshaling of your funds. This basic truth can be worked several ways.

I am going to show you the major ones in hopes you find the shoe that fits you. No discussion on the subject could be complete without bringing up the name Ralph Vince. In 1986, I ran across a money management formula for playing blackjack originally developed in a 1956 paper, "A New Interpretation of Information Rate," regarding flow of information and now called the Kelly formula by commodity traders.

What I know about math, you could add up on your thumb and first finger, but I know "math works" so I began trading commodities using the Kelly formula (see Figure 12.1). Here it is with F representing the amount of your account you will back every trade with:

$$F = [(R + 1) * (P - 1)]/R$$

P = Percentage accuracy of the system winning

R = Ratio of winning trade to losing trade

Let's look at an example using a system that is 65 percent accurate with wins 1.3 times the size of losses. The math is done as follows where P equals .65 and R equals 1.3:

$$F = [(1.3 + 1) * (0.65 - 1)]/1.3$$
$$= 2.3 * 0.65 = 1.495 - 1 = 0.495/1.3$$
$$= 38\% \text{ of account used to trade}$$

In this example, you would use 38 percent of your money behind every trade; if you had a $100,000 account you would use $38,000 and divide that by margin to arrive at the number of contracts (see Figure 12.2). If margin was $2,000, you would be trading 19 contracts.

Figure 12.1 Bond trading system without money management

System Report   *9/11/98 11:54:44 AM*

System Number: 387   Description: bonds 7/98 no bail
System Rules:
Market: Test Period: 1/1/90 to 7/16/98

┌─Summary ──┐

Trades	310	Begin Balance	$ 20,000
PL Ratio	1.4	Ending Balance	$251,813
Drawdown TT	($3,988)	Equity Peak	$251,813
Drawdown PV	–18.3%	Return	1159.1%

┌─ Profitable Trades ────────── Losing Trades ─────────────┐

Wins	230	Losses	80
Win Pct	74.2%	Loss Pct	25.8%
Win Avg	$1,350.68	Loss Avg	$985.55
Largest Win	$10,137.50	Largest Loss	($1,956.25)
Most Consec Wins	31	Most Consec Losses	6
Avg Consec Wins	4.11	Avg Consec Losses	1.45

Number of trades to reach the maximum units traded	43
Number of days to reach the maximum units traded	370

Base Unit Calculation Rules

ONE CONTRACT
ONLY

The Good, the Bad, and the Ugly of Money Management

What this formula did for my trading results was phenomenal. In a very short time, I became a real-life legend, as very small amounts of money skyrocketed. Using a percentage of the money in the account, based on Kelly divided by margin, was my approach. It was so good that I was kicked out of one trading contest because the promoter could not believe the results were accomplished without cheating. To this day, people on the Internet claim I used two accounts, one for winning trades and one for losers! They seem to forget, or not know, that in addition to being highly illegal, all trades

Figure 12.2 Varied results based on risk % of account

System Report   *9/11/98 3:06:15 PM*

System Number: 387   Description: bonds 7/98 no bail
System Rules:
Market: Test Period: 1/1/90 to 7/16/98

Summary

Trades	310	Begin Balance	$ 30,000
PL Ratio	1.4	Ending Balance	$18,107,546
Drawdown TT	($3,988)	Equity Peak	$18,107,546
Drawdown PV	–61.3%	Return	60258.5%

Profitable Trades — **Losing Trades** —

Wins	230	Losses	80
Win Pct	74.2%	Loss Pct	25.8%
Win Avg	$1,350.68	Loss Avg	$985.55
Largest Win	$10,137.50	Largest Loss	($1,956.25)
Most Consec Wins	31	Most Consec Losses	6
Avg Consec Wins	4.11	Avg Consec Losses	1.45

Number of trades to reach the maximum units traded	310
Number of days to reach the maximum units traded	0

Base Unit Calculation Rules

BASE UNITS = account balance/(draw down*2)

If Account Balance Increases by: units last trade
INCREASE units on the next trade by: 1
If Account Balance Decreases by: units last trade
DECREASE units on the next trade by: 1

must have an account number on them before the trade is entered, so how could the broker, or myself, know which trade should have the winning account number on it?

But, what would you expect, when no one to my knowledge, had turned in that type of performance ever before in the history of trading? To make matters "worse," I did it more than once. If it wasn't a fluke or luck, the losers' lament is that it must have been done by pinching some numbers or trades along the way!

What I was doing was revolutionary. And, as with any good revolution, some blood flowed in the streets. The blood of disbelief was that first the National Futures Association and then the Commodity Futures Trading Commission commandeered all my account records, looking for fraud!

The CFTC went through the brokerage firm's records with a fine-tooth comb, then took all my records and kept them for over a year before giving them back. About a year after they returned them, guess what, they wanted them back again! Success kills.

All this was due to market performance that was unheard of. One of the accounts I managed went from $60,000 to close to $500,000 in about 18 months using this new form of money management. Then the client sued me, her lawyer saying she should have made $54,000,000 instead of half a million. Now my believers were willing to put me on a pedestal, if they could collect some money. The revolution was more than anyone could handle.

What a story, huh?

But there are two sides to the edge of this money management sword.

My extraordinary performance attracted lots of money for me to manage. Lots of money, and then it began to happen: The other side of the sword flashed in the sun. Amidst trying now to be a business manager (i.e., running a money management firm) with precious few skills at doing something I am no good at anyway, my market system or approach hit the skids, with a cold streak that saw equally spectacular erosions of equity. Whereas I had been making money hand over fist, I was now losing money, hand over fist!

Brokers and clients screamed, and most took the off-ramps, they simply could not handle this type of volatility in their account balances. My own account, which had started the first of the year at $10,000 (yes, that is $10,000.00) and reached $2,100,000 . . . got hit along with everyone else's . . . it too was caught in the whirlpool, spiraling down to $700,000.

About then, everyone jumped ship but me. Hey, I am a commodity trader, I like roller coasters, is there another form of life? Not that I knew, so I stayed on, trading the account back to $1,100,000 by the end of 1987.

What a year!

Watching all this over my shoulder every day was Ralph Vince, when we were working together on systems and money management.

Long before I could see it, he saw it, saw there was a fatal flaw in the Kelly formula. I was too blind; I kept trading it, while Ralph, math genius that he is, began intense research into money management, the culmination of which are three great books. His first was *The Mathematics of Money Management*, followed by *Portfolio Management Formulas*, and my favorite, *The New Money Management*. These are all published by John Wiley & Sons, New York, and are must-reads for any serious trader or money manager.

Ralph noticed the error of Kelly, which is that it was originally formulated to assist in implementing the flow of electronic bits, then used for blackjack. The rub comes from the simple fact that blackjack is not commodity or stock trading. In blackjack, your potential loss on each wager is limited to the chips you put up, whereas your potential gain will always be the same in relationship to the chips bet.

We speculators don't have such an easy life. The size of our wins and losses bounces all over the place. Sometimes we get big winners, sometimes miniscule ones. Our losses reflect the same pattern: they are random in size. Figure 12.3 shows a trade-by-trade recap on a system I use so you can see the irregularity of wins and losses.

As soon as Ralph realized this, he could explain the wild gyrations in my equity swings; they came about because we were using the wrong formula! This may seem pretty basic in this new century, but back then we were in the midst of a revolution in money management and this stuff was not easy to see. We were tracking and trading where, to the best of my knowledge no one had gone before. What we saw were some phenomenal trading results, so we did not want to wander too far from whatever it was we were doing.

Ralph came up with an idea he calls Optimal F; it is similar to Kelly, but unlike Kelly can adapt to trading markets and gives you a fixed percentage of your account balance to bankroll all your trades. Let's look at what can happen with this general approach.

On the End of a Limb and Sawing It Off

The problem with an Optimal F approach or fixed fraction of your account is that, once you get on a roll, you roll too fast. Let me prove my point; if your average win/loss trade is $200 and you have 10 trades per month and you will increase one contract at every $10,000 of profits, it will take you 50 trades or 5 months to add that

Figure 12.3   Varied results based on risk % of account

System Report   *9/11/98 3:00:45 PM*

System Number: 387   Description: bonds 7/98 no bail
System Rules:
Market: Test Period: 1/1/90 to 7/16/98

— Summary —

Trades	310	Begin Balance	$ 30,000
PL Ratio	1.4	Ending Balance	$582,930,624
Drawdown TT	($3,988)	Equity Peak	$582,930,624
Drawdown PV	–29.7%	Return	1943002.1%

— Profitable Trades ————— Losing Trades —

Wins	230	Losses	80
Win Pct	74.2%	Loss Pct	25.8%
Win Avg	$1,350.68	Loss Avg	$985.55
Largest Win	$10,137.50	Largest Loss	($1,956.25)
Most Consec Wins	31	Most Consec Losses	6
Avg Consec Wins	4.11	Avg Consec Losses	1.45

Number of trades to reach the maximum units traded	223
Number of days to reach the maximum units traded	2152

Base Unit Calculation Rules

BASE UNITS = account balance*.15/largest loss

first additional contract. Then it will take only 2.5 months to go from 2 to 3; about 7 weeks to boost it up to 4 contracts; 5 weeks to jump to 5; one month to reach 6; 25 days, to 7; 21 days, to 8 contracts. Eighteen days later, you are at 9, and at 16.5 days, you trade a 10 lot.

Then disaster strikes, as it surely must. You have now scooted out on the end of a limb and are sitting there with lots of contracts on. Although the limb snaps when you have a large losing trade (3 times the average of $200 or $600 per contract times the 10 lot so you just dropped $6,000), you have not given back $10,000 yet. So you trade a 10 lot on the next trade and lose another $6,000. Now in two trades, you are down $12,000 from your equity high at $100,000.

The next trade is also a loser, three in a row, for the average of $200 times the 9 lot you are now trading and you get tagged for another $1,800 (let's call it $2,000). You are now down $14,000.

Meanwhile, a "smarter" trader decreases faster than you, cutting back two contracts for every $5,000 lost, so on the first hit he or she is back to 8 contracts, losing only $2,400, sidestepping another $6,000 hit, and on it goes.

And It Can Get Worse by Far . . .

Let's take a winning system. It wins 55 percent of the time, and you decide to trade 25 percent of your bankroll, starting at $25,000 on each trade. Wins are equal to losses at $1,000 each. Table 12.1 shows the way the trades played out.

You made $1,000 yet had a 65 percent drawdown while a single contract trader would have dipped $16,000 with a 20 percent drawdown!

Let's look at another scenario where we hit it right from the get-go winning 5 of 8 trades (Table 12.2), a great deal, right?

Look at this . . . 5 winners, 3 losers, and you are down. How can this be? Well, it is a combination of two things, one the money management that got you to the $58,000 also brought you down. Plus, I threw in a kicker, the last trade was just like trades the market gives us all the time, a loss 2 times greater than the average loss. Had it been the traditional loss, your account would be at $26,000. The smart trader who cut back twice the amount after the

Table 12.1	Winning 55 percent of the time	
1.	−6,000	15,000
2.	−3,000	12,000
3.	−3,000	9,000
4.	+2,000	11,000
5.	−2,000	9,000
6.	−2,000	7,000
7.	+2,000	9,000
8.	+2,000	11,000
9.	+3,000	14,000
10.	+3,000	17,000
11.	4,000	21,000

Table 12.2 A winning combination

1.	+5,000	25,000
2.	+6,000	31,000
3.	+7,000	38,000
4.	+9,000	47,000
5.	+11,000	58,000 (Wow)
6.	−14,000	44,000
7.	−11,000	33,000
8.	−16,000	13,000 What??

first loss would have lost $5,000 on trade 7, taking him to $29,000 and -$8,000 on the double hit on trade 8 to show a net of $31,000!

Looking in New Directions, Drawdown as an Asset

My trading stumbled along with spectacular up-and-down swing, while we continued looking for an improvement, something, anything that would tame the beast. From this search came the basic idea that we needed a formula that would tell us how many contracts to take on the next trade.

One such thought was to divide our account balance by margin plus the largest drawdown the system had seen in the past. This makes a lot of sense. You are sure to get hit by a similar, if not larger, drawdown in the future, so you had better have enough money for that plus margin. Matter of fact it struck me that one would need an amount equal to margin + drawdown *1.5 just to be on the safe side.

Thus, if margin was $3,000 and the system's largest drawdown in the past had been $5,000, you would need $10,500 to trade one contract ($3,000 + $5,000*1.5). This is not a bad formula, but it does have some problems.

I am now going to show several money management schemes applied to the same system. The system is one of the best I have, so the results will look a little too good. You should also notice the almost unbelievable gains the system produces, millions of dollars of profits. Now the reality is this system may not hold up in the future exactly like this. Most of you will not want to trade up to 5,000 bonds, as this test allowed, which means one tick, the smallest price change bonds can have, will cost you $162,500 if that one tick is against you. Let me add, it is not unusual for bonds to open 10 ticks against you, on any given morning, that is $1,625,000! So, don't get carried away with the profits, focus on the impact money management can have on the results.

What you should focus on is the differences in performance produced by different approaches to managing your money. The system trades bonds, which have a $3,000 margin. Figure 12.1 shows no money management; it simply reflects the complete results of the system from January 1990 through July 1998, starting with a $20,000 account balance.

Now we will take this same system and apply a variety of money management strategies so you can see which one might best work for you. To arrive at the inputs, I ran the system for just the first 7 years, then traded forward with money management for the remaining time period so the drawdown, percent accuracy, risk/reward ratios, and the like were developed on sample data and run on out-of-sample data. I allowed the system to trade up to 5,000 bonds, which is a heck of a lot.

Ryan Jones and Fixed Ratio Trading

Another friend, Ryan Jones, went at trying to solve money management like a man possessed. I met him when he was a student at one of my seminars; I later went to his seminar on my favorite subject, money management. Ryan has thought about the problem a great deal and spent thousands of dollars and research formulating his solution called Fixed Fractional Trading.

Like Ralph and me, Ryan wanted to avoid the blowup phenomenon inherent in the Kelly formula. His solution is to wander away from a fixed ratio approach of trading X contracts for every Y dollars in your account.

His reasoning is based largely on his dislike of increasing the number of contracts too rapidly. Consider an account with $100,000 that will trade one contract for every $10,000 in the account, meaning it will start trading 10 contracts or units. Let's assume the average profit per trade is $250, meaning we will make $2,500 (10 contracts times $250) and need 5 trades to increase to trading 11 contracts. All goes well, and we keep making money until we are up $50,000 with a net balance of $150,000 meaning we are now trading 15 contracts, which times $250 nets us $3,750 per win. Thus we increase an additional contract after only three trades. At $200,000 of profits, we make $5,000 per trade, thus needing only two winners to step up another contract.

Ryan's approach is to require a fixed ratio of money to be made to bump up one contract. If it takes $5,000 in profits to jump from one to two contracts, it will take $50,000 in profits on a $100,000 account to go from 10 to 11 units. The fixed ratio is that if it took 15 trades, on average, to go from one to two contracts it will always take 15 trades, on average, to bump on to that next level, unlike Ralph's fixed ratio that requires fewer trades to go to higher levels.

Ryan accomplishes this by using a variable input (one you can alter to suit your personality) as a ratio to drawdown. He seems to prefer using the largest drawdown times 2. We will now look at the same trading system for the bond market with the Ryan Jones formula.

As you can see, this approach also "creates wealth" in that it brings about an exponential growth of your account, in this case $18,107,546! However, to achieve the same growth as with the other formulas, you need to pony up a larger percentage of your bankroll on each bet. This can result in a wipeout scenario as well, unless you use a very low percentage of your money, which in return guarantees a less rapid growth in your account.

And Now My Solution to the Problem

In talks with Ralph and Ryan, I became aware that what was causing the wild gyrations was not the percent accuracy of the system, nor was it the win/loss ratio or drawdown. The hitch and glitch came from the largest losing trade and represents a critical concept.

In system development, it is easy to fool ourselves by creating a system that is 90 percent accurate, making scads of money, but will eventually kill us. Doesn't sound possible does it? Well it is, and here's how. Our 90 percent system makes $1,000 on each winning trade and has 9 winners in a row leaving us ahead by a cool 9 G's. Then comes a losing trade of $2,000, netting us $7,000, not bad. We get nine more winners and are sitting pretty with $16,000 of profits when we get another loss, but this one is a big one, a loss of $10,000, the largest allowed by the system, setting us back on our fannies with only $6,000 in our pocket.

But, since we had been playing the game by increasing contracts after making money, we had two contracts on and thus lost

$20,000! We were actually in the hole $4,000 despite 90 percent accuracy! I told you this money management stuff was important.

What ate us alive was that large losing trade. That is the demon we need to protect against and incorporate into our money management scheme.

The way I do this is to first determine how much of my money I want to risk on any one trade. I am a risk seeker so, for sake of argument and illustration, let's say I am willing to risk 40 percent of my account balance on one trade.

If my balance is $100,000 that means I have got $40,000 to risk and since I know the most I can lose is, say, $5,000 per contract, I divide $5,000 into $40,000 and discover I can trade 8 contracts. The problem is if I get two large losers in a row I am down 80 percent, so we know 40 percent is too much risk. Way too much.

Generally speaking, you will want to take 10 percent to 15 percent of your account balance, divide that by the largest loss in the system, or loss you are willing to take, to arrive at the number of contracts you will trade. A very risk-oriented trader might trade close to 20 percent of his or her account on one trade, but keep in mind, three max losers in a row and you have lost 60 percent of your money!

The final product of such a money management approach is shown in Figure 12.3. The $582,930,624 of "profits" came from determining a risk factor of 15 percent, taking that percentage of the account to arrive at a dollar amount which was then divided by the largest loss in the system.

As your account increases in value, you trade more contracts; as it declines, you trade fewer. This is what I do and this is the general area of risk I am willing to assume. It does not matter too much; a lower, and thus safer risk of 10 percent still makes millions of dollars.

What I find fascinating is that the Ryan Jones approach, which did very well, "made" only $18,107,546 while a one-contract trader would have made a mere $251,813, and my approach, at least on paper, makes a staggering $582,930,624. Clearly, how you play the game does matter, it matters immensely.

Figure 12.4 shows the system with various risk percentages being used. The graph in Figure 12.5 depicts the increase in the account equity with the increase in percent risk drawdown directly next to it. As you can see, there is a point where the amount you

Figure 12.4   Top 10 optimization results

System

Begin Balance $0.00

Ending Balance	Peak/Valley Drawdown	Risk Pct	Max Units	Restart Pct	Min Profit	Trading Style	Recover Losses	Margin
$845,429,594	−66.9%	40%	5000	100%	$0.00	All trades	No	$3,000.00
844,881,388	−77.1	50	5000	100	$0.00	All trades	No	$3,000.00
842,428,863	−72.2	45	5000	100	$0.00	All trades	No	$3,000.00
835,954,544	−61.5	35	5000	100	$0.00	All trades	No	$3,000.00
802,829,038	−54.4	30	5000	100	$0.00	All trades	No	$3,000.00
759,721,131	−46.6	25	5000	100	$0.00	All trades	No	$3,000.00
686,869,688	−38.2	20	5000	100	$0.00	All trades	No	$3,000.00
560,344,731	−28.4	15	5000	100	$0.00	All trades	No	$3,000.00
18,606	−7.0	10	5000	100	$0.00	All trades	No	$3,000.00

make rises faster than the drawdown, then as the risk percent increases, drawdown increases faster than the increase on profits in your account. This usually takes place between 14 percent and 21 percent; in most systems, any risk percent value greater than 25 percent will make more money but at a sharp increase in the drawdown.

Figure 12.5   Trading sugar

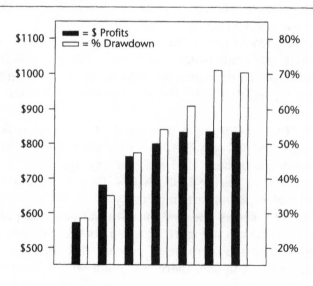

So there it is, my money management formula: (account balance * risk percent)/largest loss = contracts or shares to trade.

There are probably better and more sophisticated approaches, but for run-of-the-mill traders like us, not blessed with a deep understanding of math, this is the best I know of. The beauty of it is that you can tailor it to your risk/reward personality. If you are Tommy Timid, use 5 percent of your bank; should you think you are Normal Norma, use 10 percent to 12 percent; if you are Leveraged Larry, use from 15 percent to 18 percent; and if you are Swashbuckling Sam or Dangerous Danielle, use in excess of 20 percent of your account . . . and go to church regularly.

I have made millions of dollars with this approach. What more can I tell you—you have just been handed the keys to the kingdom of speculative wealth.

Back to Ryan and Ralph

All equity runs and money management printouts in this chapter are from ULTIMANAGER a remarkable piece of software that allows you to test money management and trade selection techniques for any system. The software will teach you about your system or approach. For examples, it will tell you if you should add more contracts after "X" number of winning or losing trades, inform you to add or subtract contracts following a big winning or losing trade, tell you what to do if you have a 70 percent accurate system that is running 30 percent on the last "X" number of trades, and on and on. If this software doesn't improve your system's performance, it can't be done. Developed by Mark Thorn, it can be purchased from Genesis Data at 800-808-3282 or by writing them at 425 East Woodmen Road, Colorado Springs, Colorado, 80919.

In any formula, even the fixed fractional approach, it is the largest loss that can kill you. Consider the results from my system with Ryan's money management shown earlier. To achieve a return even close to my formula, you would have to use a percentage of your account so high that when the large losing trade comes—and it will—you may be done in. What we need is a balance of risking but not so much that one or two very predictable events will cause too much damage. Longest losses are predictable.

chapter 13

a word in closing

In the preceding chapters, I have combined the old with the new, teaching you some of my very best long-term secrets of short-term trading. These tools and thought processes, which I have used for many years, you can now implement with the new technology of on-line and brokerless trading.

The past is indeed prologue, and the future will never be quite like the past. Never, ever. Yet you should take comfort in the following real-time trading performance. In the fall of 1998, I did the unheard of . . . I traded a one-million-dollar account in real time—real trades—in front of about 100 traders here in San Diego for a day- and short-term trading seminar I conducted, the first of its kind not only due to the amount of trading and account size, but also because I gave back a large chunk of the profits I made to my students. In that 4-day period, our actual booked profits were $225,000.

Then in 1999, assisted by Miles Dunbar, I again put on the real-time trading seminar, trading a million-dollar account once more. People came from all over the world to see what would happen. I'm certain about half of them wanted to see me lose money, the other half to see me profit—human nature at work again.

The seminar started out pretty slow; there were not many trades, only 8. For a while, the net profit figure was so small I told the students I would not include commissions in the final tally and would give them all the profits I had generated from trading so they could recoup some of their seminar costs. It was embarrassing, I had generated about $15,000 of profits in three days.

Then things started to move . . . against me; on open positions we were close to being in a negative cash position on Tuesday. Fortunately, by the time Wednesday had closed we were way in the black. Luck and all that research from the past came together as stock prices skyrocketed. We had bought the Bonds and S&P 500 on October 26, 1999, then more S&Ps on the 27th. Along the way, there were "in and out" day trades. When the dust had settled, 7 of the 8 trades made money; our net profit was $218,000 from the week of trading.

What I want to get at is this stuff works, it helps to have luck, and it sure as heck is not always perfect.

This is the background of market knowledge and technology you now can bring into the electronic Internet computerized whirlwind of online trading. We will learn more about the markets in the next few years, but scant little compared with the revolutionary upheaval just now taking place in communicating market information and trade execution.

As Bob Dylan sang in the past century, "The times, they are a changing." Just keep in mind, we'll have to as well.

My best wishes to you.

appendix a

a futures market primer

The futures market arose—as many financial instruments did—out of the need and desire to displace risk. The futures market allows producers to limit the uncertainty in their operations. To do this, they transfer the risk to willing parties who take the risk with the incentive that they, the risktakers, may make a profit off of it. This is the classic relationship between hedgers and speculators (or risktakers) that creates the liquidity of the futures market. How does this work?

A futures contract is actually a specialized forward contract, so let us begin with that. A forward contract is simply an agreement between a buyer and seller to exchange a certain amount of goods for a certain price at a certain date in the future. The motivation for this agreement on the part of the seller is that he is producing a commodity in amounts that are fixed by a general range based on, in the case of an agricultural commodity, harvested acreage, yield per acre, and so on. This seller/producer's goods will be marketable at specific times based on the seasonality of his crops, but prices for that product are constantly moving, sometimes with great volatility, creating great uncertainty as to the potential profitability of the product. The forward contract allows him to lock in prices so that he can eliminate that largely external uncertainty of price and focus on the more controlled uncertainties of the operating of his business.

What does the buyer get out of it? In the case of a basic forward contract, the buyer will generally be a producer requiring the commodity as an input in the production of its own product. For example, a pig farmer would buy corn for feed, or a flour mill would buy from a wheat farmer. In this case, the buyer is also trying to eliminate the external uncertainty of the price of his input. In this case, both parties find the agreement mutually beneficial, and both can proceed in their respective businesses without worrying about losing money based on the price of the commodity itself.

But what happens, if for some reason, either the buyer or the seller wants to break the contract? As harvest time approaches, the farmer's crops are beset by a plague of parasites, and the farmer realizes that production will fall short and that he will not be able to hold up his end of the bargain. What are his options? He could break the contract, but that would create all sorts of legal trouble, not to mention the damage it would do to his customer relations. Another answer is he could buy an amount equal to the shortfall from another producer. But from whom? A neighbor perhaps. But maybe his neighbor was hit by the same infestation and is trying to cover a forward position as well. So now our farmer has to go out and find someone who is expecting to have an excess equal to his shortfall at the same time in the future as he needs it. This is a tall order for someone whose business is the producing of a commodity, not the purchasing of it. Enter the futures contract.

Futures contracts solve many of the problems involved in making and breaking forward contracts. They do this through standardization. Having defined a specific quality, size, and delivery date of the standard contract for a particular commodity, it becomes much easier to make or break a forward contract because everyone is speaking the same language. But standardization alone does not solve all liquidity problems. There is still the issue of finding a buyer when one is interested in selling, or finding a seller when one is interested in buying. For example, our farmer in the example above, places an ad in a trade magazine: "Wanted: 3 Contracts of December No. Yellow Corn. Bids call xxx-xxx-xxxx." At the same time, he may scan the magazine for advertisements from sellers. Effectively, the magazine provides the marketplace, but it is not exactly a very liquid marketplace as purchases and sales will take at least as long as it takes to get out one issue. So is there a better way to create a marketplace? Yes, and that is how we arrive at exchanges.

Once a standard contract specification is established, it is possible to set up an exchange that breaks the connection between buyers and sellers in all given transactions. This is done by having the exchange fulfill a clearing function whereby all contracts are bought from the clearinghouse and all contracts are sold to the clearinghouse. In this way, buyers and sellers can be assured that they will always have a ready, willing, and able counterparty to effect any transaction at any time. Just as important, the clearinghouse function makes it possible to exit from a forward agreement by making an offsetting transaction because the clearinghouse will have an account that shows the net effect of any purchases or sales for a given client. So now, our farmer who is trying to make up for his shortfall, can put in a call to his broker to buy 3 contracts at the market. These three contracts offset the amount of corn he would have otherwise come up short.

Now, instead of selling 10 contracts to A, producing 7 contracts worth, buying 3 more contracts from B, receiving the 3 from B, shipping the 10 to A, our farmer can sell 10 contracts to the clearing firm, buy 3 contracts from the clearing firm, and deliver the 7 contracts to the clearing firm's warehouse. Thus our farmer does no direct business with anyone but the exchange, and the number of physical transactions of corn are reduced to only one. This is how standardized, exchange-traded futures contracts improve efficiency of the commodities market.

But as individual traders who are neither a supplier of any commodity, nor a producer of any product that uses any commodities as inputs, what is our function in the market? We are the speculators, and our role is essential to the exchange because we provide the liquidity. We are the ones who step in to buy when the hedgers want to sell and sell when the hedgers want to buy. We are there to take the risk when everyone else is trying to get rid of it. Rather than locking in a price and making profits from the resulting sale, we attempt to profit from the price change itself.

Let's say that the plague that hit our farmer is not just a local phenomenon. It is a countrywide problem, so crop estimates are way down. Farmers all over the country are trying to cover their short positions, but there is no one to buy from because they are all buyers and there are no sellers. Enter the speculator who believes that the parasite scare is unwarranted: The natural predators of the parasites are thriving and will soon grow in number and gobble up all the crop-destroying vermin. We sell into the buying frenzy as prices skyrocket. Why? Because we expect estimates to go back up as soon as this ecological balancing act starts to take place. Farmers will then try to lock in prices on the corn that they didn't think they would grow. Prices start falling as the farmers enter the market with new short sales. We close out our short positions with offsetting long transactions (i.e., we make purchases of future goods to counteract the sales of future goods that we made during the scare). Thus, as speculators, we profited from the volatility of the market, while keeping that market liquid when there was a perceived shortage of supply.

This is a very simple explanation of how and what a speculator does, but the basics hold: Speculators do not intend to deliver or take delivery on the commodity in which they trade. As such, there are many varieties of speculators. Some base their trading solely off the news, supply and demand, and other fundamental factors. Then there are those who try to interpret price action whether through chart patterns or psychology, or both.

The Mechanics of Trading

Now that we have covered the basics of the industry, let's look at some of the mechanics of trading. When you buy or sell a futures contract, you do not pay or receive payment for it at that point. Only during a contract's settlement period do long and short parties pay or receive payment in full for the goods rendered. However, when you buy or sell a futures contract, you are required to put up a good-faith deposit on that contract. This deposit is known as original margin, and its size depends on the exchange. In some cases, a broker will require more than the exchange minimum, depending on the client or the nature of the commodity at the time (e.g., a broker may ask for more margin from an undercapitalized client on a commodity in a particularly volatile period).

The concept of margin is what allows futures traders to leverage themselves much more than if they traded other instruments. This leverage, however, can cut both ways, leading to profits or losses very quickly. For example, you put up $1,000 margin to buy a $10,000 contract of JuJuBees. Two days later, JuJuBees are trading at $11,000 a contract. You close out your position and realize a gain of $1,000 on your $1,000 investment. 100 percent. That is pretty exciting stuff—a pretty good return for two days of work. What happens though, if instead of going up, JuJuBees go down to $9,500?

You decide to play it safe and cut your losses by closing your position with a sale. The contract price has only gone down 5 percent, but your $1,000 has turned into $500. A 50 percent loss. That is leverage.

Because you were only required to put up 10 percent of value of the contract—or ⅒th—your gains or losses accrued at 10 times the change in price. Contract goes up 10 percent, you gain 100 percent. Contract goes down 5 percent, you lose 50 percent. So what happens if the contract value dips to $9,000 and your original investment is wiped out? Can you stay at the table? I wouldn't recommend it. But if you wanted to, you would be asked by your broker to put up what is known as maintenance margin. To maintain your position, you need to add to your good-faith deposit. The maintenance margin required and the levels at which it is needed are set by your broker, who will usually use the exchange minimums as a guideline.

In the same vein, if you have an unrealized profit on a trade (i.e., a winning position that you haven't closed out), that profit is debited to your account and can be used as margin for other trades.

The concept of leverage works for both long and short positions. In the preceding example, we were long JuJuBees. If we were short one contract, though, things would have been very different. For one thing, that 10 percent increase in price would have meant a 100 percent decrease in our equity. The 5 percent decrease? A 50 percent *increase* in our equity. Leverage cuts both ways and it cuts deep. That is why futures trading has such a notorious reputation for volatility. It is not the price moves, but rather the leverage that makes it such a wild ride.

appendix b

recommended reading

These days, you can find a wide selection of books on trading in any large bookstore. Back when I got going, information was much more difficult to come by. The books that were out there often didn't make it into stores. They were too expensive (demand was high, supply was low so . . . voilà) for bookstores to shelve them so you had to go to specialty retailers and catalog accounts. Those sources still exist despite the proliferation of trading books at Barnes & Noble, Borders, Amazon.com, and all the others. At the bricks-and-mortar chains, you can peruse a book before buying it, making the process easier in one sense, but these stores sometimes don't get the books shelved in the right places. Or the sales staff doesn't know its Gann from its Fibonacci. Consequently, if you are looking for a particular topic, it is sometimes easier to work through a catalog house like Trader's Press or Trader's Library. What follows are some recommendations for the further exploration of the world of trading. There is so much depth of knowledge in this field, you should be able to learn something new (and potentially profitable!) in each one of these books. But don't limit yourself. But don't just take everything at face value, either. Read much, and read critically.

Against the Gods—The Remarkable Story of Risk, **Peter L. Bernstein**
Although not a book on trading, this book has inspired more trading ideas than any other book. It traces the history of our interpretation

of risk and how we have tried to overcome it. A must for any trader's library.

The Compleat Day Trader and The Compleat Day Trader II, Jake Bernstein
These books are classics from one of the industry's long-standing educators. Jake gives a great mix of material from the very general (i.e., using systems and psychology together to trade effectively) to the very specific (i.e., how to spot entry and exit points).

Complete Guide to the Futures Markets, Jack Schwager
Covering fundamentals, technicals, spreads, and everything you can think of, this is an essential reference or front-to-back read. The math can get a little heavy going at times, but is well worth your effort.

Cybernetic Trading Strategies, Murray Ruggiero
This is one of the best systems development and testing books out there.

Day Trader's Manual, William Eng
A classic. Trade the markets intraday as you would long term and you are begging for trouble. Eng gives you an inside track to understanding some of the shortest of short-term concepts.

The Definitive Guide to Commodity Trading, Vols. I and II, Larry Williams
A comprehensive two-book series that helps both newcomers and seasoned traders learn how to implement systematic approaches to trading. Large sections on volatility and picking market turns help clarify the mysteries of the markets.

Design, Testing and Optimization of Trading Systems, Robert Pardo
Pardo gets down to the nitty-gritty of building and perfecting your own computerized trading system. Concise. No matter what software you are building your system on, this book can help.

Four Cardinal Principles of Trading, Bruce Babcock
Bruce was a legend, and this is one of his greatest contributions. He reduced success in trading down to its most elemental parts—identifying trends, cutting losses, maximizing profits, and managing risk.

Getting Started in Futures, **Todd Lofton**
This simple introduction to futures is a great way to go further in-depth as to how the system works. The more you learn about the mechanics, the more you can take advantage of the system. There isn't a whole lot of trading advice in here, but as a concise description of what it is all about, this book is very good.

Getting Started in Technical Analysis, **Jack D. Schwager**
Schwager, author of *Market Wizards* and *New Market Wizards,* has written a simple yet very effective introduction to this extremely broad topic.

How I Made a Million Dollars Trading Commodities, **Larry Williams**
An oldy but goody. The timeless techniques described in this book are still used and work in today's markets. Uncover the mysteries of open interest and price patterns.

Intermarket Technical Analysis, **John Murphy**
In the book you have in your hands, I introduced you to intermarket analysis. Remember how we used Bond futures to confirm our S&P trades? Well, if you want to dig deep into that concept, John Murphy has written the best book out there on the subject.

The Intuitive Trader, **Robert Koppel**
For those who think that trading is more art than science, Koppel could help you develop the techniques to "feel" the market better.

The Investor's Quotient, **Jake Bernstein**
One of the best books on psychology in trading the futures markets. If you don't read any other psychobabble, mumbo-jumbo, check this one out. It is right on from a guy who knows whereof he speaks.

Japanese Candlestick Charting Techniques beyond Candlesticks, **Steve Nison**
Candlesticks are a chart format all their own. I didn't go into them in this book, but they can be used to identify powerful patterns in the futures markets. Steve Nison takes you step by step through this time-tested technique and helps to marry it with Western methods of chart analysis.

Live the Dream by Profitably Day Trading Stock Futures, Gary Smith
Gary Smith is one of the industry's champs. You can learn a lot from a guy who had 10 consecutive years of winning trading. Chock-full of techniques, you'll also find excerpts from his trading diary. A great view from the middle of the fog of battle.

The Mathematics of Money Management, Ralph Vince
I mentioned this book in chapter 12; I think it should be on every trader's shelf (and its principles in every trader's plan). Effective money management is essential to successful trading, and Vince will get you going in the right direction.

The New Science of Technical Analysis and New Market Timing Techniques, Thomas R. DeMark
Tom is one of the greatest innovators in the field, and these two books are an important contribution to the trader's library. Indicators galore!

Schwager on Futures: Technical Analysis, Jack D. Schwager
This is a much more fleshed out version of his *Getting Started in Technical Analysis.* When you are ready for the next level, check it out.

Seasonality, Jake Bernstein
Another great offering from Bernstein, this time giving insight into discovering profitable seasonal trades.

Spread Trading, Howard Abell
Rather than profiting off the advance or decline of the price of a futures contract, you can bet on the convergence or divergence of different contract prices that are generally correlated. This is called trading spreads, and Howard Abell's book is a good start in that direction.

Sure Thing Commodity Trading, Larry Williams
Over a dozen detailed methods for trading specific markets. Also includes a section on seasonality and how to profit from spreads.

Technical Analysis of the Futures Markets, John Murphy
Some call it the Bible. It is a comprehensive text with all the major technical tools. He makes some of the most difficult indicators

understandable, and generally does a good job of presenting the material.

Trading without Fear, Richard Arms, Jr.
Fear and greed are the driving elements of the markets. They are what make us do all the wrong things. Learn not to succumb to these impulses using the understanding you can find in Richard Arms's classic.

The Trading Game, Ryan Jones
Ryan Jones is a leading light in the area of money management. Read this book and profit.

Trading for a Living, Alexander Elder
Alex Elder has educated tens of thousands of traders with this book. He is one of the granddaddies of education and this book is comprehensive, covering psychology, trading tactics, and money management. Written long before the Internet changed everything, this book still has a lot to give. Check it out to learn what it is *really* like to trade for a living.

Trading 101 and Trading 102, Sunny Harris
Concise, readable, effective. These two books teach you all the basics, including setting yourself up as a business. Lots of practical tips from an industry vet.

Trading Systems and Methods, Perry Kaufman
This book is currently in its third edition, and it just keeps getting better. The most comprehensive discussion of trading systems, this book belongs on every trader's shelf. Go to it for trading ideas and you will find them.

Trading to Win, Ari Kiev
For those that need to learn to keep their emotions out of their trading, this book outlines a step-by-step, goal-oriented approach to taming your fear and greed and sticking to your trading plan.

index

Want Larry to teach you how to day trade?

For more information on trading with
Larry Williams, write to him at:

P.O. Box 8162
Rancho Sante Fe, California 92067

or visit him on the Web at:
ctiming.com

CPSIA information can be obtained
at www.ICGtesting.com
Printed in the USA
BVHW030226181219
567044BV00004B/10/P